Working With ‿

A Joint Venture for the New Century

COUNCIL *on*
FOREIGN
RELATIONS

Independent Task Force Report No. 73

Charles R. Kaye and
Joseph S. Nye Jr., *Chairs*
Alyssa Ayres, *Project Director*

Working With a Rising India
A Joint Venture for the New Century

Task Force Members

Task Force members are asked to join a consensus signifying that they endorse "the general policy thrust and judgments reached by the group, though not necessarily every finding and recommendation." They participate in the Task Force in their individual, not institutional, capacities.

Alyssa Ayres*
Council on Foreign Relations

Ajay Banga*
MasterCard

C. Fred Bergsten
Peterson Institute for International Economics

Marshall M. Bouton*
Chicago Council on Global Affairs

Nicholas Burns
Harvard University

Stephen P. Cohen*
Brookings Institution

Richard Fontaine
Center for a New American Security

Sumit Ganguly*
Indiana University, Bloomington

Helene D. Gayle
McKinsey Social Initiative

Charles R. Kaye
Warburg Pincus LLC

Mary Kissel*
Wall Street Journal

Joseph S. Nye Jr.
Harvard University

Gary Roughead
Hoover Institution

Mariko Silver
Bennington College

Ashley J. Tellis*
Carnegie Endowment for International Peace

Member, ex officio
Robert D. Blackwill
Council on Foreign Relations

*The individual has endorsed the report and signed an additional view.

Contents

Foreword

Eighteen years ago, I chaired a Council on Foreign Relations–sponsored Independent Task Force on South Asia, *A New U.S. Policy Toward India and Pakistan*, which was followed up by a second Task Force report one year later after both India and Pakistan tested nuclear weapons. Rereading those reports serves to remind how two decades ago nonproliferation was the dominant lens through which Washington viewed its interests in India and South Asia. Today, with the end of the Cold War, the emergence of terrorism with a global reach, a long war in Afghanistan, the rise of China, and India's economic growth, there is the reality of a much wider aperture.

U.S. relations with India have changed as well. Bilateral ties are closer than ever, including on sensitive strategic matters. India conducts more military exercises with the United States than with any other country, and increasingly, New Delhi and Washington confer on a wide range of issues, including global health, cybersecurity, clean energy, and democracy promotion. Prime Minister Narendra Modi has given special emphasis to India's ties with the United States, having just completed his second visit to this country, and having welcomed President Barack Obama to India's Republic Day parade, a first for a sitting U.S. president. Prime Minister Modi has made economics the cornerstone of his foreign policy, and has stated his goals of achieving faster economic growth and reducing the hurdles to doing business in India.

That said, many of the issues that previously limited the U.S. relationship with India remain, albeit to a lesser degree. While Washington and New Delhi have converged more closely on Asia-Pacific strategic matters and counterterrorism, Indian leaders do not always see Washington's global policy goals as congruent with their interests, especially regarding Iran and the Middle East. Indian policymakers also remain ambivalent about the market-based, open competition that has potential to power their economy and expand the U.S.-India economic relationship.

In some ways, it is possible to speak of two Indias—one of great accomplishment and promise, another that never quite lives up to its potential. It is similarly possible to speak of two U.S.-India relationships, one that broadens and deepens, another marked more by mutual disappointment and frustration. It is against this backdrop that the Council on Foreign Relations launched this Task Force—the first to focus exclusively on India—to assess the current situation in India and the U.S.-India relationship, and to develop findings and recommendations for U.S. foreign policy.

This report urges U.S. policymakers to reframe the terms they use in crafting a partnership with a rising India that does not seek an alliance relationship with the United States. It recommends seeing U.S.-India ties more as a joint venture. This term has specific meaning. As in business, joint ventures do not presuppose agreement on every matter outside those objectives. Narrowing and managing those inevitable differences will be critical to the U.S.-India relationship.

The Task Force offers a limited, prioritized set of additional recommendations. Among the most important for U.S. policymakers is the call to support India's economic growth. Making this the top priority for U.S.-India relations will require the United States to rethink its economic approach to India. The report offers steps to do so, including supporting Indian membership in the Asia-Pacific Economic Cooperation forum, completing a bilateral investment treaty, starting high-level discussion of bilateral sectoral agreements, crafting a long-term pathway to a free trade agreement or Indian membership in the Trans-Pacific Partnership, and further increasing defense trade.

The Task Force also urges Indian leaders to deepen their country's economic liberalization, something essential if India is to achieve sustained high growth rates. On strategic matters, the Task Force commends the recent expansion of defense ties, and urges renewed attention to homeland security and counterterrorism cooperation. Looking at the region, the Task Force recognizes the challenge to U.S.-India relations posed by U.S. policy toward Pakistan, as well as the drag on India's rise presented by the risk of conflict with Pakistan. The Task Force recommends that India—for the sake of its own future—pursue an improved relationship with Pakistan. In parallel, the Task Force urges the United States to demand that Pakistan tackle terrorism, and prepare to cease U.S. funding for defense sales and coalition support funds should Pakistan prove unwilling. The report also makes recommendations about priorities for collaboration on global issues, recognizing the cyber domain and global health as those with the greatest potential.

I would like to thank the Task Force's co-chairs, Charles R. "Chip" Kaye and Joseph S. Nye Jr., for their thoughtfulness, expert guidance, and commitment to producing a report that would result in real action by policymakers in both countries. I also thank the accomplished group of Task Force members and observers whose insights and knowledge contributed so much to the final product.

I am grateful to Chris Tuttle, managing director of CFR's Independent Task Force Program. His steady hand has been instrumental to the Task Force process. I would finally like to thank Project Director and Senior Fellow for India, Pakistan, and South Asia Alyssa Ayres for helping to guide the deliberations and drafting the important report that they produced.

Richard N. Haass
President
Council on Foreign Relations
November 2015

Acknowledgments

Seven years ago, in 2008, I served as project director of a Task Force on U.S. relations with India sponsored by the Asia Society. Our deliberations overlapped with the momentous completion of the U.S.-India civil nuclear agreement. It seemed at the time as if Washington and New Delhi had conquered the disagreements of the past and could only aim higher together. Our report envisioned an expansive partnership with India, one in which both countries' governments and private sectors could—and would—collaborate.

Cooperation grew closer, and across more areas. India and the United States elevated formal diplomatic consultation to a Strategic Partnership, and President Barack Obama declared support for Indian permanent membership in a reformed United Nations Security Council. But at the same time, the global economic crisis, slowing growth in both countries, strategic divergences over the Arab uprisings, challenges in Afghanistan and Pakistan, and particularly acute trade spats resulted in unanticipated turbulence for U.S.-India ties. In December 2013, when an Indian consular official was arrested in New York, India and the United States experienced a diplomatic rupture that lasted several months.

In India, the May 2014 election of Prime Minister Narendra Modi's government ushered in a "reset" for the country, economically as well as diplomatically. Washington and New Delhi have gotten back on track. Three summit-level meetings between Obama and Modi have taken place; once again, bilateral prospects look promising. This Independent Task Force spent six months deliberating over ways to keep U.S. relations with India looking promising, identifying ways to better conceptualize what it means to partner with a proud rising power, and thinking through how to best prioritize the most crucial areas for collaboration. The report that resulted here reflects concentrated effort by the dedicated members and observers of the Task Force, and I am deeply appreciative of the time they gave and the talents they lent to this project.

It was a privilege and pleasure to work so closely with Task Force co-chairs Charles R. "Chip" Kaye and Joseph S. Nye Jr., both of whom brought the historical memory of longtime India watchers to the Task Force mandate. Most important, their global perspectives on matters economic and strategic ensured that the questions we asked—and attempted to answer—were contextualized against larger global trends and India's role within that broader landscape. Both devoted many hours to the Task Force, leading meetings, reading and reviewing numerous drafts, and ensuring a refined set of priorities. Their colleagues Margaret Grunow and Jeanne Marasca helped coordinate us all. Chip additionally led a small delegation, co-led by Task Force member Marshall M. Bouton, to Mumbai and New Delhi in August. That intensive trip provided insights that shaped the report in significant ways. Many thanks to everyone who shared their views with our delegation; their input shaped the way the Task Force decided to narrow its findings and recommendations.

We also received helpful input from many CFR members. The Washington Meetings team organized an event in Washington, DC, to discuss some of the report's findings and recommendations in progress, which Task Force member Nicholas Burns led with me. Thank you to Nick for making the trip down from Boston for the discussion, and to the CFR members who offered their diverse recommendations.

CFR's Publications team did a superb job editing the report and bringing it to publication; CFR's Communications, Congress and U.S. Foreign Policy Program, Corporate, National, Outreach, and Washington teams all helped amplify the reach. CFR's Events teams in New York and Washington deserve plaudits for coordinating all of our meetings and events smoothly.

Chris Tuttle and Veronica Chiu of CFR's Independent Task Force Program were central to this project from conception to completion, from the initial inklings through the selection of Task Force members, the meetings, the August trip to India, and then the work of reviewing numerous drafts. I am grateful to them for their camaraderie and support. My research associate Ashlyn Anderson deserves special thanks, especially for the role she assumed as Task Force rapporteur and organizational stalwart during our August trip to Mumbai and New Delhi.

In addition, Marisa Shannon and intern Alexandra Smith of CFR's Independent Task Force Program also provided valuable assistance.

Above all, I am grateful to CFR President Richard N. Haass for seeing this moment as opportune for examining U.S. relations with India through an Independent Task Force, as well as to CFR Senior Vice President and Director of Studies James M. Lindsay, both of whom gave me the opportunity to direct this effort.

Alyssa Ayres
Project Director

Acronyms

APEC	Asia-Pacific Economic Cooperation
BRICS	Brazil, Russia, India, China, and South Africa
GDP	gross domestic product
ICANN	Internet Corporation for Assigned Names and Numbers
ILO	International Labor Organization
IMF	International Monetary Fund
IT	information technology
NATO	North Atlantic Treaty Organization
PPP	purchasing power parity
TPP	Trans-Pacific Partnership
UNDEF	United Nations Democracy Fund
UNDP	United Nations Development Program
WTO	World Trade Organization

Independent Task Force Report

Executive Summary

Call it an American consensus: India now matters to U.S. interests in virtually every dimension. India's economy is a fast-growing emerging market, increasingly important for international business, and Indian businesses have become investors in the United States. Geopolitically, India's growing military capabilities can help protect the sea lanes and deliver humanitarian assistance quickly throughout the South Asian region, and increasingly across the greater Indo-Pacific. India's long-standing stability anchors the volatile Indian Ocean region and helps ensure that no single power dominates the Asia Pacific, leading to a stable balance of power. India's sheer scale means that complex global challenges, such as climate change, cybersecurity, and health, cannot be solved without it. Additionally, India's diverse, plural democracy stands out in a world in which authoritarianism poses new threats to the interests of the United States and its allies.

Today, India has a window of opportunity for significant change. There are two Indias, one that appears poised for global success, and one that continues to struggle with weighty economic, social, and developmental challenges. Both exist at the same time—but against the backdrop of slowing global growth, India has a greater chance to stand out. With Prime Minister Narendra Modi elected to office on a campaign focused on job creation and economic growth rather than the welfarism of the past, India may at last be able to translate its long-heralded power potential into reality.

In light of this potential for change in India, and with the 2016 presidential election gearing up in the United States, the Council on Foreign Relations (CFR) sponsored an Independent Task Force on U.S.-India relations to examine developments in India and weigh those against U.S. foreign policy. Successive U.S. administrations have worked to improve ties with India, but even with the high-level focus on strategic partnership, the relationship has encountered difficulties. The Task

Force considered India's current political and economic preoccupations and its ambitions for the next decade, reflected on how those mapped onto U.S. national interests, and developed a slate of findings and recommendations for the United States (and to a limited extent, India) to consider.

FINDINGS

1. India's shift away from nonalignment remains incomplete, but continued geopolitical changes around the world, the importance of economics, and China's rise have all created a landscape in which Indian and U.S. interests are in a process of *structural realignment*. The Task Force finds that this structural realignment increases opportunities for the United States and India to pursue mutual self-interest through closer cooperation.

2. The Task Force finds that if India can maintain its current growth rate, let alone attain sustained double digits, it has the potential over the next two to three decades to follow China on the path to becoming another $10 trillion economy. This places India at a unique moment in which the right choices could propel it to far greater relevance for global gross domestic product (GDP) growth in the decades to come. Consequently, nothing is more important to India's future success—across all facets of national power—than achieving sustained high levels of annual economic growth.

3. Because of the *combined* economic, national security, and global policy potential India presents, the Task Force finds that a rising India offers one of the most substantial opportunities to advance American national interests over the next two decades.

4. The Task Force finds that for India to realize its ambitions, for its society as well as its economy, it will need to tackle barriers that hold back women and girls.

5. The Task Force finds that India risks being left behind in international trade. India has reached a turning point and will have to decide whether it wants to become a major part of global trade flows and deeply integrated into global supply chains. Doing so would boost India's efforts to grow its manufacturing sector and its economy; choosing not to will make that ambition harder to achieve. India

might become an outlier to major trade flows—and the opportunity they bring—if it chooses to remain apart from the arrangements being put in place by the ambitious sectoral and regional trade negotiations under way. Opening more fully to global trade and investment will allow the Indian economy to draw upon the external resources necessary to shift its economy into the higher gear it seeks.

6. The Task Force finds that Indian ambivalence about the role of markets and open competition—and therefore a more limited role for government intervention—will continue to constrain its economic growth.

7. The Task Force finds that barriers to a much deeper relationship continue to exist, tied to U.S. policy toward Pakistan. Indian officials remain skeptical that the United States can ever fully be trusted as a security partner when they see Washington appear to acquiesce to Islamabad's continued inaction on terror groups that have targeted India and the United States. Indian officials also view with skepticism the sale of defense equipment Washington authorizes to Pakistan.

8. Pakistan has innumerable problems independent of its issues with India. India is poised for power and prosperity if it can remain focused on its domestic transformation, and the risk of conflict with Pakistan threatens to drag India down. India should not have to, nor should it want to, endure further decades of having its strategic options limited by Pakistan.

9. The Task Force finds that U.S. policy toward Afghanistan has created particular difficulties in the U.S.-India bilateral relationship due to the increasing threat of greater instability resulting from internal Afghan divisions, the many violent threats to the country's stability, and the drawdown of U.S. and other external forces. New Delhi also fears that what it perceives as American eagerness to extricate itself from the region could lead to more influence on the part of China and Pakistan.

10. The Task Force finds that defense ties and strategic consultations have progressed well compared with the past but still have much room to grow. Cooperation can develop much further along both the strategic-operational as well as the defense-industrial and technology tracks. Homeland security and technical counterterrorism cooperation has begun but not progressed as deeply as it could.

11. In cybersecurity and in global health, India has advanced technical capabilities and large, highly capable talent pools with experience working seamlessly with American partners, as has been demonstrated in the information technology (IT) and medical industries. The Task Force finds that India and the United States share significant interests—and unique capabilities—in both cyber and health issues, which offer the capacity for potentially transformative bilateral cooperation.

12. The Task Force finds little likelihood that India's development pathway and domestic political dynamics would permit its government to change its views on a commitment to legally binding emissions frameworks anytime soon.

13. The Task Force finds that, as the world's two most populous democracies, India and the United States should be obvious partners in work to share lessons from and promote democracy elsewhere in the world.

RECOMMENDATIONS

1. India's size, its class-of-its-own sense of self, and its fierce independence all make for a bilateral relationship—both today and tomorrow—that little resembles American ties with other countries. India does not sign on to formal alliances and does not seek one with the United States. To capture this opportunity for increased cooperation while acknowledging the inherent limits to partnership with India, the Task Force recommends that U.S. policymakers explicitly emphasize a "joint-venture" model for U.S.-India relations, focused on a slate of shared pursuits on which interests converge—and with clear mechanisms for coordinating and managing the known and expected disagreements. The strategic convergence between Washington and New Delhi, including on the Asia Pacific, should not be construed as directed at any other country and is not an alliance against China.

2. Recognizing that India's success is inherently in U.S. interests, the Task Force recommends that Washington and New Delhi transform their economic relationship just as significantly as the civil nuclear agreement transformed their strategic ties in the previous decade.

U.S. policymakers should elevate support for India's economic growth and its reform process to the highest bilateral priority, committing to ambitious targets for bilateral economic ties along with clear steps to get there. This will require a shift in U.S. government strategy toward India.

3. Similarly, the Task Force recommends that the government of India increase the pace and scope of economic liberalization with the goal of expanding markets, including opening the Indian economy more deeply to trade and foreign investment. The Task Force urges Indian political leaders, in both government and the opposition, to coalesce around a reform agenda, persuade their publics of its urgency, and implement with dispatch.

4. To reduce the chances of conflict that could delay or hinder India's global rise, the United States should encourage India to improve its relationship with Pakistan—as an investment in its own rise—particularly, at least to start, through greater trade connectivity. As important, the United States should demand that Pakistan meet its obligations as a state to tackle terrorism emanating from its territory, in both India and Afghanistan. If Pakistan is not willing to rein in terror, Washington should be prepared, at minimum, to end U.S. taxpayer funding for defense equipment sales and reimbursement of coalition support funds.

5. The Task Force recommends that the United States extend its commitment to Afghanistan—even beyond President Obama's decision to slow the withdrawal of U.S. troops from Afghanistan and retain a force of some 5,000 U.S. troops in the country into 2017. The United States should commit to a doctrine stating that future decisions regarding the size, scope, and timeline for deployment of U.S. forces will be determined by on-the-ground realities and not artificially imposed schedules, and without a declared date of departure. Such a move would help assure India and others that U.S. actions will not undermine the goal of long-term regional stability. The United States should also continue to reinforce India's helpful role in development, infrastructure, and diplomacy with Afghanistan, ensuring that India is a standing member of regional consultative mechanisms focused on Afghanistan.

6. The Task Force recommends that the U.S. government, building on the consultation and increasing levels of interaction in recent

years, invest further attention in the security relationship with India across the entire spectrum. Homeland security and counterterrorism cooperation should receive added emphasis.

7. Regarding global issues, in the cyber domain, multilateral Internet governance cooperation has progressed well in 2015 and should continue. Bilateral collaboration should move beyond consultation to focus on more robust law enforcement cooperation, joint training, warning, and heightened security to continually upgrade protection for this critical infrastructure. As with their collaborations in the clean energy space, India and the United States should create signature joint ventures in global health.

8. On climate change, Washington should continue to impress upon New Delhi the urgency of emissions action, pressing India to commit to improve its energy intensity or declare a per capita income level at which it would be willing to cap emissions, if it cannot commit to emissions caps at present. Doing so would signal India's commitment on the world stage. But given India's domestic political constraints, Washington should emphasize collaboration through technical consultation on matters like grid capacity, energy efficiency, automobile fuel efficiency, and financial tools to mobilize domestic capital for electricity-sector investment. Consultations on civil nuclear energy should continue. In recognition of the practical reality of India's development pathway, Washington should revise its policy, which at one time promoted technical assistance for clean coal but no longer does.

9. The United States should approach India as a frontline partner on technical training and capacity building for democracy around the world.

Introduction

India is the world's largest democracy, managing its multireligious, multiethnic, and multilingual diversity at an unprecedented scale. It is a growing emerging market that is increasingly a destination for international business, and Indian businesses have gone global with endeavors in every region of the world. If it can maintain high rates of growth, India will become the world's third-largest economy at market exchange rates within a decade. India has established itself as a land of low-cost innovation, growing through ideas and entrepreneurship, changing the shape of international commerce, and becoming an increasingly important center for global corporate research. It is a member of the Group of Twenty and seeks a permanent seat on the UN Security Council, which President Barack Obama has endorsed.

That is one India. Another exists at the same time.

Despite India's growing wealth, it has the largest number of poor in the world—one-third of the world's 1.2 billion people living in extreme poverty.[1] India's population will soon overtake China's. India faces enormous challenges of education, training, and human development. It also faces daunting infrastructure needs, estimated at $1 trillion over the next decade. Some 25 percent of Indians lack access to electricity—more than 304 million people, concentrated across rural areas.[2] Corruption scandals have captured the headlines in recent years and brought governance concerns to the fore in politics. Internationally, even as it rises as a world power, India continues to see itself as a leader of the global south. India is a tough—indeed, difficult—voice on global trade, at times willing to scuttle global consensus, and without a clear idea about whether openness will help or harm its economy. India also sees itself as an exceptional power, a sui generis nation unique in its own way, and for that reason is not often persuaded by precedents elsewhere.

During the Cold War years, the United States and India had a fraught relationship. The United States saw itself as the leader of the free world, and India, despite its democracy, positioned itself as a leader of the Non-Aligned Movement. But, as has been well documented, the end of the Cold War and India's economic reform process created once-in-a-generation structural changes in world politics. Indian strategic thinkers began to see an opportunity for their country to emerge as a major power. They also started to see the United States, with its economic and technological might, as a way to leverage India's rise. The United States, too, sought a new relationship with India. In 2005, Washington and New Delhi overturned decades of mistrust with the initial announcement of a civil nuclear agreement. The process established a new strategic partnership. Many in the United States began to see India as a U.S. *ally*, a natural partner with shared values, including democracy, pluralism, and freedom of speech. **India's shift away from nonalignment remains incomplete, but continued geopolitical changes around the world, the importance of economics, and China's rise have all created a landscape in which Indian and U.S. interests are in a process of *structural realignment*. The Task Force finds that this structural realignment increases opportunities for the United States and India to pursue mutual self-interest through closer cooperation.**

Successive U.S. administrations have bet on India, seeing its rise and its emerging capabilities as squarely aligned with U.S. national security interests. Call it an American consensus: India now matters to U.S. interests in virtually every dimension of geopolitics. India's growing military capabilities can help protect the sea lanes and deliver humanitarian assistance quickly throughout the region, as its leading response to the Nepal earthquake and the evacuations from Yemen demonstrated this year. India's long-standing stability anchors the volatile Indian Ocean region and helps ensure that no single power dominates the Asia Pacific, leading to a stable balance of power. Given India's sheer scale, complex global challenges such as climate change, cybersecurity, and health cannot be solved without it. And in a world in which authoritarianism poses new threats to the interests of the United States and its allies—with Russia under Vladimir Putin for the foreseeable future, and China under Xi Jinping escalating activities in the South China Sea, cyber arena, and elsewhere—supporting democracy will be of even greater importance to U.S. interests.

Today, India has a window of opportunity for significant change. With Prime Minister Narendra Modi elected to office after a campaign focused on job creation and economic growth—not the sops and welfare promises typically seen as vote-getters—India may at last be able to translate its long-heralded power potential into reality. It is the first time in India's history that a national election featured a campaign about economic growth, which also means that if Modi cannot deliver on growth and jobs, public disillusionment may result in Indian politics reverting to its usual ways. The window for making the reforms needed to unleash high rates of growth may not be open forever, which makes this moment all the more decisive.

Over the last year, the Indian economy has regained momentum after a slow period from 2011 to 2014, when annual GDP growth dropped as low as 5.1 percent. India's 7.5 percent growth rate this year also stands out against slowing global growth. In fact, India's growth has surpassed China's this year, making it the fastest-growing major economy in the world. **The Task Force finds that if India can maintain its current growth rate, let alone attain sustained double digits, it has the potential over the next twenty to thirty years to follow China on the path to becoming another $10 trillion economy. This places India at a unique moment in which the right choices could propel it to far greater relevance for global GDP growth in the decades to come. Consequently, nothing is more important to India's future success—across all facets of national power—than achieving sustained high levels of annual economic growth.** The natural corollary to that observation lies in the opportunity India's economic growth presents for global prosperity.

Because of the *combined* economic, national security, and global policy potential India presents, the Task Force finds that a rising India offers one of the most substantial opportunities to advance American national interests over the next two decades. The United States and India should not miss the opportunity to close the gap between where U.S. relations with India could go and where they are at present. The Task Force does not make such a sweeping aspirational statement lightly and recognizes the many potential hurdles along the way.

Despite the seeming convergence of interests, progress in the U.S.-India relationship—played out over the years in many chapters—has been a bumpy ride. Viewed from a U.S. perspective, India has not always delivered on the expectations some American policymakers, lawmakers, and business leaders have of the relationship, and it is clear that a multiparty consensus within India on the type of relationship it would like with the United States is still evolving. Although the United

States and India have dramatically expanded the range of areas in which they collaborate over the past decade and substantially overcome legacy problems, the relationship still has enormous room for enhancement. Problems during 2013 and 2014, particularly over trade and the arrest of an Indian diplomat in the United States, revealed continued fragilities.

Contrary to expectations, the inauguration of the Narendra Modi government has resulted in a reset of U.S.-India relations following recent difficulties. Many in India and the United States alike anticipated that Modi, given the history of his visa revocation in 2005, might prioritize Japan and China as India's leading partners and sideline the United States. Instead, he has embarked upon an invigorated personal foreign policy in which the United States appears to have a central role. Given his personal signal of greater interest in ties with the United States, and with the 2016 U.S. presidential race already under way, CFR sees this moment as ripe for ambitious thinking on U.S. relations with India. CFR thus decided to sponsor an Independent Task Force to take stock of the present, assess India's domestic and foreign policy trajectories, and develop findings along with recommendations on U.S. foreign policy toward India. It is the first occasion in which CFR has sponsored an Independent Task Force focused solely on India, not South Asia broadly—in and of itself recognition of India's importance.

Background

How should Washington think about India's trajectory, and its ties with a country changing so rapidly? The Indian government conceptualizes its policy horizon in terms of at least a decade. In the view of the Task Force, the United States should look toward a similar time frame in developing and executing its India policies. U.S. interests have much staked on the power India is likely to—but has not yet—become, so it is worth some explication of where trends suggest India will be headed.

India has undergone dramatic transformation over the past ten years. The most important structural factor has been economic growth. In 1994, the Indian economy was smaller than that of the Netherlands and Australia, at number fifteen using market exchange rates. In 2004, India had not broken into the top ten global economies; at number twelve, it lagged behind Canada, Mexico, and South Korea. By 2014, according to the International Monetary Fund (IMF), the Indian economy crossed the $2 trillion threshold (figure 1), making it the ninth-largest economy globally at market exchange rates. In purchasing power parity (PPP) terms—useful for comparing relative welfare across countries, but less helpful for assessing economic might—India has already overtaken Japan as the third-largest economy (figure 2).[3]

However, when examining GDP per capita—a much better indication of the sophistication of an economy—the picture looks much different (figure 3). India's GDP per capita, estimated by the IMF at $1,808 for 2015, puts the country in the bottom third.

The IMF projects that the Indian economy will grow healthily at around 7.5 percent annually through 2020, the last year for which projection is available.[4] India's finance ministry has declared its ambition for a $5 trillion economy by 2025, a goal theoretically achievable based on current projections if India can maintain at least a 7.5 percent or higher rate of growth. But India will need to grow sustainably in the 8 to 10 percent range to create enough jobs, reduce poverty further, and establish India as a true global economic leader.

FIGURE 1. TEN LARGEST GLOBAL ECONOMIES, GDP
(CURRENT PRICES), 2014 DATA IN U.S. DOLLARS (BILLIONS)*

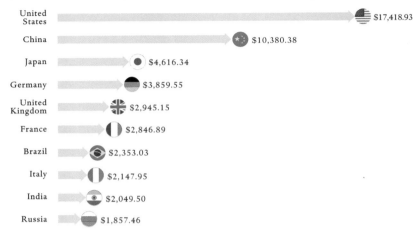

*IMF estimates for China, Germany, Russia

Source: International Monetary Fund World Economic Outlook Database, 2015.

FIGURE 2. TEN LARGEST GLOBAL ECONOMIES, GDP (PPP),
2014 DATA IN U.S. DOLLARS (BILLIONS)*

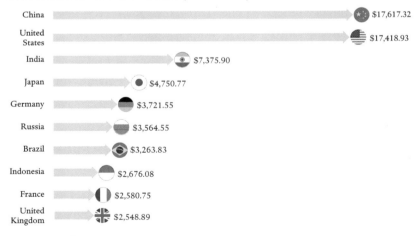

*IMF estimates for China, Germany, Russia

Source: International Monetary Fund World Economic Outlook Database, 2015.

FIGURE 3. GLOBAL ECONOMIES, GDP PER CAPITA (CURRENT
PRICES), 2015 ESTIMATES IN U.S. DOLLARS (BILLIONS)

Source: International Monetary Fund World Economic Outlook Database, 2015.

Indeed, Indian policymakers target 8 to 10 percent growth over the coming decades, as China has done, to deliver domestic transformation faster. Growth of that scale would meaningfully affect global GDP, just as occurred with China. India's GDP currently accounts for 2.65 percent of global GDP (6.82 percent in PPP), some distance from the 13.3 percent of global GDP China's economy represents. But it is getting closer to Germany's 4.95 percent contribution.[5] As the Indian economy grows, it has the potential to become increasingly indispensable for global prosperity—becoming an engine of growth for its region and its trading partners, and rising as a source of global investment.

India's economic growth has been accompanied by falling poverty. Growth, thanks to the first-generation economic reforms begun in 1991, has lifted 133 million people out of extreme poverty into the next rung up—low-income status—over the decade from 2001 to 2011. Estimates about the size of India's middle class vary, ranging from a high of more than half a billion by 2025, which would make India the world's "fifth-largest consumer market by 2025," to more conservative estimates—down to a low of a little over thirty million people.[6] But few dispute the future potential for explosive growth in India's middle class, precisely because India has such a large population, began its economic reforms about twelve years after China, has had less consistent reform, and thus lags in similar transformation. The prospect for consumer markets in India to play a far larger role in global economic growth—and offer increasingly greater opportunity for global companies—is linked closely to middle-class expansion and rising disposable incomes.

Just as U.S. investment in India helps grow the Indian economy, Indian purchases of U.S. exports and Indian investment in the United States help the U.S. economy and create jobs. As one of the focus countries of the U.S. National Export Initiative, India has already become a significant export market for U.S. goods and services. As U.S. Secretary of Commerce Penny Pritzker noted in September 2015, "Our exports to India support more than 180,000 American jobs."[7] Further, the globalization of Indian companies has benefited the United States as India became one of the fastest-growing sources of inbound investment to U.S. shores. A recent survey of one hundred Confederation of Indian Industry member companies revealed that their investments alone in the United States exceeded $15 billion and created more than ninety-one thousand jobs across all fifty U.S. states.[8] This trajectory is set to increase as India becomes more prosperous.

CHALLENGING HEADWINDS

India's transformation depends on tackling formidable challenges. As the economy has grown, so has its population. India currently has 1.3 billion people and is on track to exceed China's population by 2022, several years earlier than previously projected (figure 4). This brings potential opportunity, but along with it India must overcome significant liabilities for its population bulge to avoid becoming a burden. Unlike other countries at its income level, India has grown through services rather than manufacturing. Successive Indian governments have identified the need to expand India's manufacturing sector to create more jobs than the services sector can provide. Modi has unfurled an international "Make in India" campaign around a call to global manufacturers to site new factory operations in India.

India's future demographics also merit comment. Nearly half the country is younger than twenty-five, and India will remain young

FIGURE 4. INDIA AND CHINA POPULATION GROWTH,
2015 TO 2050 (BILLIONS)

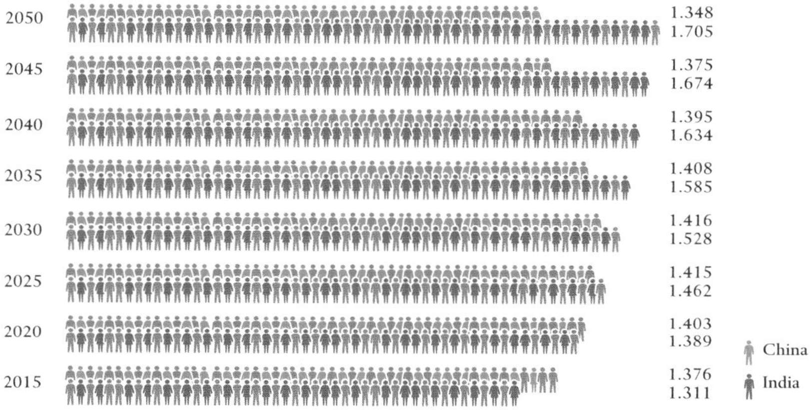

2050		1.348 1.705
2045		1.375 1.674
2040		1.395 1.634
2035		1.408 1.585
2030		1.416 1.528
2025		1.415 1.462
2020		1.403 1.389
2015		1.376 1.311

China
India

Source: United Nations Department of Economic and Social Affairs, Population Division, World Population Prospects, 2015 Revision.

through the first half of this century. By 2020, India will be the youngest country in the world, with a median age of twenty-nine, and could soon have one-fifth of the world's working-age population. India's enormous workforce-age population will peak only in 2050 (figure 5), so it has decades during which it needs to lay the groundwork for what is widely termed its demographic dividend.[9] The pursuit of realizing the dividend from India's demographic trajectory—preparing India's hundreds of millions coming of workforce age with employable skills—has become a major focus for successive Indian governments.

In mid-July 2015, the Modi government launched a new initiative, Skill India Mission, designed to create the training infrastructure to prepare four hundred million people with job-ready skills by 2022. Here, too, Indian ambitions are global. Modi declared India's goal of becoming "the human resources capital of the world." Just looking at the demographics, time matters: India will have to succeed soon in a mass educational undertaking; otherwise, its youth bulge will likely create domestic woe rather than global opportunity.

Recent survey data also reveals a surprising and unwelcome trend in India. Female workforce participation rates dropped dramatically between 2004 and 2010, according to the International Labor Organization (ILO), dipping from around 37 percent in 2004–2005 to 29

FIGURE 5. INDIA'S FUTURE DEMOGRAPHICS—TOTAL POPULATION BY MAJOR AGE GROUP

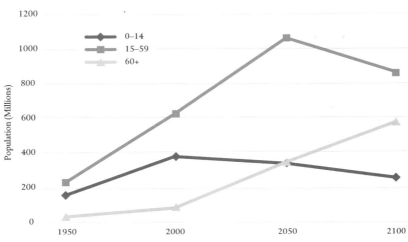

Source: United Nations Department of Economic and Social Affairs, Population Division, World Population Prospects, 2015 Revision.

percent in 2009–2010. The data showed declines "across all age groups, across all education levels, and in both urban and rural areas," which puts India nearly at the bottom of the 131 countries covered (eleventh to last).[10] IMF Managing Director Christine Lagarde has advocated "urgent remedies" to boost female labor force participation.[11] India has certainly seen women reach the top of their fields, including as prime minister, and the remarkable cohort of some dozen female chief executive officers in India's financial services industry, but the larger data showing lagging female workforce participation is undeniable.

Estimates of the benefits to national economies from improving gender parity indicate the potential for huge gains in India. The McKinsey Global Institute released a study in September 2015 that contained estimates of a best-case "full potential" parity-for-women scenario in India. Their conclusion: economic parity for women could add as much as 60 percent to the Indian economy in 2025 versus following a "business-as-usual" path. Even if India were to match the "best-in-region" scenario, rather than the "full potential" ideal, gains would still be a 16 percent boost to the Indian economy of 2025 compared with a status-quo path. Based on McKinsey's figures, that represents a range from $0.7 trillion to $2.9 trillion in gains, using 2014 dollars.[12]

In addition, India continues to wrestle with violence against women and incomplete enforcement of laws that prohibit practices harmful to girls and women, such as child marriage, female infanticide, and rural "courts" known as *khap panchayats*. Indian civil society has become particularly active in advocating for justice following the December 2012 gang rape of a young student, an act of violence so shocking that it made headlines around the world. Civil society pushed lawmakers to pass a much-strengthened rape law and create fast-track courts so cases would not pend in perpetuity. And Modi used his inaugural Independence Day address in 2014 to speak frankly to the country about the ills of gender discrimination, marking the first time an Indian prime minister has addressed female infanticide so prominently and bluntly. These are social issues that Indian citizens are consciously working to improve, aware of the magnitude of work remaining. In addition to its importance as a matter of justice under India's own laws, overcoming gender-based violence, as with female workforce participation, will deliver gains to the Indian economy. A recent World Bank study that examined on a global scale the economic costs of gender-based violence found that it ranged from "1.2 percent to 3.7 percent of GDP."[13]

The Task Force finds that for India to realize its ambitions, for its society as well as its economy, it will need to tackle barriers that hold back women and girls. Overcoming these challenges will bring gains to the Indian economy.

India's struggle to ensure full participation of women in national life points to an important issue India will need to redress to achieve its ambitions. There are others. Despite its rapid growth and the wealth creation of the past fifteen years, India remains a lower-middle-income country, home to one-third of the world's extremely poor. Growth has been accompanied by rising inequality, though India's Gini index—a method of scoring income distribution, with higher numbers indicating greater income inequality—at thirty-four remains below the United States' (forty-one) and China's (thirty-seven), based on World Bank data.[14] Inequality across castes, religions, and other social groups also remains a concern for Indian policymakers, as do urban-rural disparities. Caste protests linked to affirmative action policies resurfaced during 2015. India's chief economic advisor, Arvind Subramanian, noted in the 2014–2015 *Economic Survey* that India remains at the bottom of its Brazil, Russia, India, China, and South Africa (BRICS) cohort in rankings like the United Nations Development Program (UNDP) Human

Development Index.[15] Its per capita income at market exchange rates is $1,808 (2015 estimate), about one-fifth of China's.[16]

The World Bank estimates that 47 percent of India's population still works in agriculture, based on 2012 data, but the sector has yet to experience the nationwide reforms that could link it more deeply with world-class supply chains, free up farmers to negotiate contracts with large wholesale buyers, and create the markets needed for the sector to increase productivity. Although employing a plurality of India's citizens, agriculture contributes just 17.6 percent to India's GDP, industry 29.7 percent, and services the majority, at 52.7 percent.[17] This inverted pyramid of people employed versus contribution to GDP illustrates precisely the urgent challenge India faces as it transitions to a more urban, less agricultural way of life.

India's urbanization has increased from a little more than 27 percent in 2001 to more than 31 percent as of the 2011 census. Subramanian noted in the 2014–2015 *Economic Survey* that "as many as thirty-five cities in India had a million-plus population. At current rates of growth, urban population in India is projected to reach 575 million by 2030."[18] This trajectory illustrates both an economic and infrastructural challenge—building out cities at a scale never previously envisioned—and a cultural one as well. India has long imagined itself as rural, its traditional ways of life conceptualized as the "real India." The real India of the future will be increasingly urban at the same time.

India's infrastructure deficit will require huge investment, estimated at $1 trillion over the course of the next decade. Roads, trains, bridges, airports, urban railways, power grids, clean water, and sanitation—all must be either upgraded or built to accommodate India's rapidly growing cities as well as to better link small towns and rural areas with large population centers. The larger infrastructure deficit has been well known for quite some time—see McKinsey & Company's reports urging acceleration in infrastructure development since at least 2009, for example—but India has been slow to tackle this enormous requirement. Half the population lacks adequate sanitation, and the Modi government has made building toilets, especially for girls, a signature undertaking in its larger push to raise sanitation standards nationwide.

On social indicators, India is doing better than in the past but still has considerable distance to travel. The most recent census of India, in 2011, revealed an increase in literacy levels, from 65 percent to 74 percent, but India will need to focus on further increasing overall literacy rates if the country is to equip its large youth demographic to perform in the global economy. Although it has shrunk over the past decade, a gender gap in education continues. India's male literacy rate of 82 percent still substantially exceeds its female literacy rate of 65 percent. How India meets its education challenge, especially for girls, will be the single most important determinant in successfully turning its growing population into a "resource for the world," to paraphrase Modi. Indeed, how India meets its obligations to its citizens in creating economic growth, providing opportunity for gainful employment, and augmenting infrastructure to support a twenty-first century economy will determine whether India can finally overcome the liabilities of long-standing struggle.

INDIAN FOREIGN POLICY AND INDIA'S DOMESTIC CONCERNS

On the global stage, despite India's move into the ranks of the top ten global economies, India's leaders continue to see their country as part of the developing world, not as the world's third-largest economy in PPP terms. This self-perception shapes Indian policy choices in international institutions and has tended to constrain Indian ambitions globally. Against this economic and demographic backdrop, the world's largest democracy has become increasingly focused on achieving the domestic transformation that would provide jobs—seeking to employ an estimated one million new entrants to the workforce each month—and lift those at the bottom of the pyramid out of poverty. Achieving that economic transformation will require both becoming more open to the world and instituting second-generation reforms focused purely within India—including land acquisition, labor, agriculture, and capital and financial markets—and easing red tape more generally. India ranks 130 of 189 countries in the 2016 World Bank Ease of Doing Business index, an indication of the burdensome environment. The latter set of issues revolves around India's positioning in global trade flows and its approach to foreign capital on Indian soil. India is not as protectionist as it once was, but it remains far from being a completely open market economy.

The intersection of India's domestic imperatives with its approach to international economic policy has led in some cases to sharp divergences between Washington and New Delhi, or more precisely, between New

Delhi and many countries around the world. India and China together ended the 2008 World Trade Organization (WTO) Doha Development Round discussions over concerns about protection for their countries' farmers. The negotiations remain at a standstill. India's temporary derailment of a global agreement to facilitate trade in 2014 reaffirmed its ambivalence about the benefits of trade and greater openness. Moreover, the Indian government has begun an internal review of all current free-trade agreements previously negotiated, under the belief that it has not benefited as much as it should have from trade. India remains outside the four major plurilateral sectoral agreements currently under negotiation: the new Environmental Goods Agreement, the Agreement on Government Procurement, the now-concluded expansion of the Information Technology Agreement, and the Trade in International Services Agreement. And although the United States and eleven other countries have concluded negotiations on the Trans-Pacific Partnership (TPP) trade pact—with rumblings of China's interest in joining beginning to percolate in Washington—there have been no signals from India in finding a pathway to membership, apart from its renewed interest in joining the Asia-Pacific Economic Cooperation (APEC) forum, a required stepping-stone.

The Task Force finds that India risks being left behind in international trade. India has reached a turning point where it will have to decide whether it wants to become a major part of global trade flows and deeply integrated into global supply chains. Doing so would boost India's efforts to grow its manufacturing sector and its economy; choosing not to will make that ambition harder to achieve. India might become an outlier to major trade flows—and the opportunity they bring—if it chooses to remain apart from the arrangements being put in place by the ambitious sectoral and regional trade negotiations under way. Opening more fully to global trade and investment will allow the Indian economy to draw upon the external resources necessary to shift its economy into the higher gear it seeks. Participation could bring great benefits: C. Fred Bergsten of the Peterson Institute for International Economics estimates possible gains to India from participation in an expanded TPP at around $500 billion in exports and $200 billion in national income. On the other hand, remaining outside an expanded TPP would not only forfeit those gains but also result in an estimated loss of another $50 billion due to trade diversion to competing countries, creating a substantial opportunity cost of $550 billion to exports. This is an opportunity India should not lose.[19]

On the strategic side, India has been slowly modernizing its military, an expensive process supported by the growth of the economy. The United States has been a beneficiary of New Delhi's slow shift toward equipment diversification; although Russia had been India's sole supplier during the Cold War decades, the decision to opt for more partners has helped boost U.S. military sales to India from essentially zero to around $13 billion over the past fifteen years. Service-to-service exchange has increased dramatically. As widely cited, India now conducts more military exercises with the United States than with any other country.

Strategic consultations have increased as well. Washington and New Delhi now have a convergence of interests on South Asia and the Asia Pacific, on maritime security in the Indian Ocean, on Africa, on counterterrorism broadly, and on strategic (nuclear) stability matters. India has been less active, however, on issues concerning the Middle East and its growing instability—in fact, India opted not to join the global coalition against the self-proclaimed Islamic State, for example—and has generally favored a status-quo approach to crises. India has been a strong development partner for Afghanistan but has grave concerns about the direction stability in the region may take, especially against the backdrop of the Afghan government's negotiations with the Taliban, which Washington and Beijing have endorsed. On this most sensitive question of the region's future, and with a smaller presence of U.S. forces scheduled now for 2017, a divergence with Washington on both strategy and tactics has raised questions in New Delhi about U.S. partnership.

THE MODI EFFECT

During his first year in office, Modi placed great emphasis on foreign policy. He has traveled extensively—receiving some criticism in India for it—and raised India's global profile, just as the Bharatiya Janata Party election manifesto had promised. The Modi foreign policy prioritizes stability and space in India's immediate region through consolidation of ties across South Asia, although challenges still remain with Pakistan, and deepening its interactions across Asia, called an Act East policy. As importantly, the Modi foreign policy places great emphasis on developing a network of economic relations as a central instrument for furthering India's economic growth. Although South Asia remains the least economically integrated region in the world, the Modi government, building on efforts made by its predecessors, has expanded trade and economic ties with Bangladesh, Nepal, and Sri Lanka, but has had less success with Pakistan. Modi's highest-profile foreign visits have involved announcements of major investments in India—such as his trip to Japan, which resulted in a Japanese pledge of $35 billion in public and private investment and financing, or his trip to the United Arab Emirates, which resulted in a $75 billion pledge for investment in Indian infrastructure.

India is in the process of reorienting its position on the world stage, which requires rethinking a long-standing foreign policy that has been defensive, focused on nonalignment and its successor, "strategic autonomy."[20] Indian Foreign Secretary S. Jaishankar has called for India's transition from a "balancing" to a "leading power," even asking, "Are we content to react to events or should we be shaping them more, on occasion even driving them?"[21] This shift from a focus on nonalignment, which in practice kept Washington at arm's length, to an approach that emphasizes Indian global leadership, opens the door further for Washington and New Delhi to deepen ties. It also primes India to take on a larger global role.

U.S.-India Relations: A Reformulation for the Future

Democratic and Republican U.S. administrations from President George H.W. Bush forward have sought to improve relations with India. Washington has a strong interest in better relations with New Delhi for many reasons—the pursuit of mutual goals, complex global issues, the economic power India is becoming, and the strategic convergence on Asia. Beyond the government-to-government level, business and trade ties have grown substantially over the past fifteen years, arguably the single-biggest bilateral change and one uniquely important to strengthening ties across the board. The growing Indian American community, now numbering around three million, has kept India visible on the political and business agenda in the United States and has risen to ever-higher levels of accomplishment at the top of virtually every field.

But India is not yet top-of-mind for most Americans. According to a 2014 Chicago Council on Global Affairs public opinion survey, on a scale of one to one hundred, with the highest number a "warm, favorable feeling," Americans viewed India as a fifty-three.[22] That compares favorably with China (forty-four), but unfavorably with close allies like Canada (seventy), the United Kingdom (seventy-four), or Germany (sixty-five)—illustrating the problem that although India might be important for the future of the United States, Americans are not yet thinking about India with as much affection as they are about more established relationships. Further, a 2015 Chicago Council on Global Affairs public opinion survey revealed that just 34 percent of Americans felt "a great deal" or "a fair amount" of confidence in India's ability to "deal responsibly with world problems," although a 63 percent majority wanted to see India play a larger role in the world.[23]

In addition, people-to-people exchange between the United States and India is extremely asymmetric, with migration flows moving from India to the United States for work or education and much less in the other direction. This tracks closely with recent Pew Research Center public opinion findings: the United States enjoys a 70 percent favorability rating in India.[24] Annual surveys of foreign students in the United States consistently show large numbers of Indian citizens coming to the United States for higher education, hovering around one hundred thousand (figure 6).

Heading in the other direction, American students simply do not venture in large numbers to study in India (figures 6 and 7). In part, the asymmetry in these flows of students lies in the fact that India's population is nearly four times larger than that of the United States. But Americans in general have not seen India as a top ten destination for learning or economic opportunity. (Note that tiny Costa Rica attracts nearly twice the number of American students as India.) This will likely change over time, but it is worth noting as a marker of the relative place India currently occupies in the American imagination compared with other countries.

In the business world, attention to India has blossomed from almost nothing to a healthy interest. India's economic growth created opportunities within India, for Indian citizens and Indian companies, and for American corporations and investors as well. In the process, India's growth created new American constituents invested in India's success. The U.S.-India Business Council, for example, grew from an anemic sixty-some members in the late 1990s to more than two hundred by 2008, and around 330 today. U.S.-India bilateral trade has crossed $100 billion in goods and services—a fivefold increase from $19 billion in 2000. But to put it in a global context, that $100 billion is only around one-sixth of U.S.-China trade. This contrast, though potentially disheartening, points to the opportunity ahead.

During and immediately after World War II, the United States was India's major defense infrastructure builder because the British were unable to address the problem. But suspicion and a chimerical desire for self-reliance in defense production led then Prime Minister Jawaharlal Nehru to sever the American connection. Until the early twenty-first century, U.S.-India strategic and defense ties were marked by mutual hostility and suspicion. Over the past fifteen years, ties have gone from limited interaction and no significant technology-procurement relationship to one of extensive exercises, around $13 billion in defense equipment sales, regular civil-military consultation, and an ambitious vision for coproduction and codevelopment of advanced defense equipment.

FIGURE 6. STUDY ABROAD FIGURES FOR U.S. STUDENTS IN INDIA AND INDIAN STUDENTS IN THE UNITED STATES

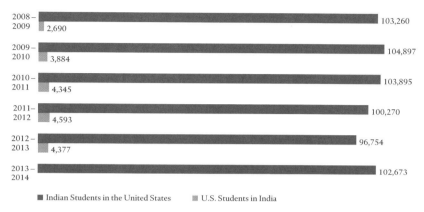

- ■ Indian Students in the United States
- ■ U.S. Students in India

Note: Comparable data for U.S. students studying in India is not yet available for 2013–2014.

Source: Institute of International Education (2008–2014), "Top 25 Places of Origin of International Students, 2008/09–2013/14," Open Doors Report on International Education Exchange.

FIGURE 7. LEADING DESTINATIONS OF U.S. STUDY ABROAD STUDENTS, 2012–2013

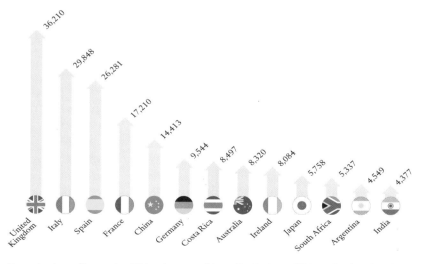

Source: Institute of International Education, 2014, "Top 25 Destinations of U.S. Study Abroad Students, 2011/12–2012/13," Open Doors Report on International Educational Exchange.

New consultations with India on homeland security preparedness began in 2011, enhancing the counterterrorism consultation already in place; now, consultations on cybersecurity and strategic space matters occur as well.

The U.S.-India relationship today covers a far wider range of areas than at any time in the past. U.S. Ambassador to India Richard R. Verma noted in early June that the U.S. embassy in New Delhi is currently tracking seventy-seven initiatives resulting from the January 2015 Obama-Modi summit.[25] Bilateral initiatives centered on technology collaboration in particular, such as clean energy, health research, and civilian space collaboration, have advanced quickly and without problems.

Despite such progress, India is not yet among the closest U.S. partners for immediate consultation on global crises, a role still occupied by members of the North Atlantic Treaty Organization (NATO) and U.S. allies in Asia, such as Japan and Australia. To put it simply, India is not a frontline global partner, not among the top five countries Washington policy officials would call immediately to coordinate on any urgent global issue. India and the United States have not yet collaborated together on any crisis in the United Nations, for example, and on some of the most challenging questions in the Middle East and with Russia, India has been silent. Moreover, U.S. and Indian interests are not fully aligned on these tough questions.

In addition, difficulties in U.S.-India relations during 2013 and 2014 offer the lesson that despite advances, ties between the two countries have not yet attained a solid footing to ward off crises. From a U.S. perspective, it is not entirely clear how strong a relationship India's policymakers would like to see with the United States— at least in the terms Americans are accustomed to when thinking about close strategic partners. Washington, for example, looks to its closest partners for endorsement—or at least not overt rejection—of American policy positions. This expectation has resulted in disappointment in Washington when Indian officials appear to embrace positions that Americans see as impossible to understand, such as during Russia's invasion of Ukraine. In India, on the other hand, a strong sense of policy independence creates a context of à la cartism for New Delhi's relationships.

A CHANGING WORLD, NEW OPPORTUNITIES

As noted, clear bipartisan consensus exists in the United States about the importance and desirability of a deeper relationship with India, which the Task Force believes offers one of the most significant opportunities to advance a combination of U.S. interests in the coming decades. But India's size, its class-of-its-own sense of self, and its fierce independence all make for a bilateral relationship—both today and tomorrow—that little resembles American ties with other countries. India does not sign on to formal alliances and does not seek one with the United States. To capture this opportunity for increased cooperation, while acknowledging the inherent limits to partnership with India, the Task Force recommends that U.S. policymakers explicitly emphasize a joint-venture model for U.S.-India relations, focused on a slate of shared pursuits on which interests converge—and with clear mechanisms for coordinating and managing known and expected disagreements. The strategic convergence between Washington and New Delhi, including on the Asia Pacific, should not be construed as directed at any other country, and is not an alliance against China. Just as joint ventures in business bring together parties to advance a shared objective without subordinating their many other interests, so should India and the United States pursue their shared ambitions without assuming that each will see eye to eye with the other on every matter. Reframing ties in this way will better explain how convergence on the need for open sea lanes, for example, may not presume agreement on climate change, and how convergence on the Asia Pacific may not presuppose like-mindedness on the Middle East. Such a conceptual recalibration, concentrating on a series of specific collaborations rather than a diffuse appeal to bonhomie that creates disappointments of its own, allows more opportunity for success and should help insulate against disillusionment. Reframing ties with this flexible model will also create conceptual space for inevitable disagreements without calling into question the basis of the partnership or unintentionally "infecting" other issues. It will also facilitate better management of disagreements because the expectation will be that divergences inherently exist and, therefore, must be managed.

A direct note about alliances is in order. The United States has built strong and durable alliances with North American, European, and

Asian partners, and tends to see alliances as the highest, most desirable form of partnership. This is not the direction that U.S.-India relations are headed; India has clearly indicated it does not seek the obligations that come with alliances, viewing that as an unacceptable constraint on its freedom of action. That said, the world is not static. Should international politics shift further—if the structural realignment under way should progress further—and should a future India, a "leading power," elect to seek a more alliance-like relationship with the United States, the Task Force would endorse that ambition. The limits to the relationship at present are placed by India and its sensitivity to the inherent inequality any alliance with a superpower presupposes. Thus, our recommendations proceed from that reality.

To shift the bilateral relationship toward a framework focused on joint ventures, Washington should, as a matter of practice, do the following:

- Invest more time and attention in developing the habits of cooperation that support stronger ties. Consultations should go beyond the institutionalized and highly scripted formal dialogues and expand to include informal, routinized, pick-up-the-phone consultation that American officials regularly employ with the closest U.S. partners. Senior officials, at the principals and deputies levels in Washington, should make a regular and frequent habit of speaking with Indian counterparts—not on the eve of an emergency vote, or to arm-twist on a matter previously decided in consultation with other partners—but as a matter of sustained, weekly or biweekly international consultation toward policy formulation.

- Consider designating, with the imprimatur of the White House, a specific senior official (subcabinet-level or higher) for whole-of-government authority on India policy, someone charged with responsibility for advancing long-term U.S. interests with India, no matter what myriad other short-term crises elsewhere compete for policymakers' time and attention. In previous administrations, the deputy secretary of state or the undersecretary for political affairs has played this role.

- Build protective insulation around the inevitable disagreements that will continue to arise by creating predictability: flagging problems early on; providing routinized high-level channels of redress and discussion; and allowing for better coordination and management of those differences, including how to discuss problems publicly (or not), in shared or coordinated language.

Similarly, to make this joint-venture model work, New Delhi will need to be prepared to

- commit internal resources to policy formulation in advance—not at the last minute—to better facilitate active, detailed consultation on issues in depth and with multiple U.S. officials involved; and to
- adopt a more flexible approach to diplomatic protocol and hierarchy, given that the rank structure of Indian ministries does not correspond equally with the much larger and more differentiated U.S. systems.

Although a joint-venture model will not prevent disagreements, it should, at the very least, better protect successful initiatives from negativity arising from policy disagreements elsewhere, because neither side will expect support from the other on every matter. The focus instead becomes furthering the successes of defined joint ventures while working to minimize, or at least contain, the inevitable disagreements.

The next question becomes how to prioritize among the ever-expanding areas of collaboration to accomplish more together on matters of greatest significance.

Priorities for the Joint-Venture Future

AN ECONOMIC GROWTH AGENDA

If India is to realize its ambitions as a global power, it will need to deliver sustained economic growth over decades. Washington has endorsed India's desired trajectory, seeing India's rise as convergent with U.S. interests. Therefore, supporting that rise means backing an economic growth agenda for India. It will mean finding avenues to enhance India's economic transformation that leverage U.S. strengths while also carefully hiving off some particularly tendentious hotspot issues for further dialogue.

Increased economic growth is the most important factor for India's future—the underpinning of Indian strategic power, the basis for an India that can deliver on its global ambitions, and a critical component of a maximally effective U.S.-India partnership. As outlined earlier, India's most urgent challenge is to create an economic engine that makes India's large, rising youth demographic a blessing rather than a burden. Absent consistent growth at rates of 8 percent or higher, India cannot fulfill its promise as a global power in the near term. An India that can grow at the 10 percent rates China has experienced over the past three decades will transform itself faster as a power on the world stage. This will be impossible for India to do without export-driven growth. Achieving India's own ambitions will only happen with continued economic reform in India and a willingness to join decisively the world of free and open trade.

In this context, the Task Force finds that Indian ambivalence about the role of markets and open competition—and therefore a more limited role for government intervention—will continue to constrain its economic growth. Although the scope and pace of India's economic reforms are to be determined by India's citizens and government, the Task Force notes that slower or stalled reforms will ultimately dampen India's growth potential, trade and commercial ties with India's trading partners, and interest in investment in India. The instinct to protect parts of the Indian economy, coupled with remaining bureaucratic hurdles that make doing business harder in India than in other countries, prevents India from fully drawing on the external investment support and growth in trade that could boost the economy. What is more, continued ambivalence will limit the growth of business community well-wishers with a deep interest in and attention to India's success. Here, one need only note the support that the U.S. business community lent to the U.S.-India civil nuclear agreement to see why a cohort of supporters matters for achieving political goals. By contrast, continued reforms toward open competition and improved ease of doing business in India will free the economy for greater growth. Reform will further lead to larger and more engaged U.S. constituencies that have stakes in India's success because it will create success for them as well. Therefore, economic ties have the potential to be the leading edge of the U.S.-India relationship—a self-reinforcing virtuous circle of support—but that depends on a positive business climate in both countries.

Modi's election has assuaged some anxieties about India's economic openness but against the backdrop of a country that still has "second-generation reforms" to undertake. Modi entered office with ambitions to transform the Indian economy and create jobs for the country's large youth demographic but has bumped up against the current of Indian politics long accustomed to populist measures as vote-getters. Instead of delivering transformative reforms in tax policy, land acquisition, and labor laws during his first year in office, the Modi government is finding itself looking for incremental changes and devolving reform down to the states. India's own political economy—one of a raucous democracy—has already made this much harder than it would be in an authoritarian state, and it will take time. But greater urgency on this front among India's leaders is needed to spur the Indian economy toward the conditions needed for sustained high growth, apart from the external liberalization needed to boost trade flows further. Unlike previous economic reform efforts in India, typically cast as technocratic measures under duress, that the Modi government campaigned on growth and market-based job creation provides greater political heft for economic liberalization than ever before.

Multilaterally, India's conflicted views on open competition have positioned it on the sidelines of major efforts to ease trade barriers and facilitate commerce. As noted, India's positions do not signal readiness to embrace a global and open trading system without reservations. The United States recently concluded negotiations on a regional free-trade agreement with eleven other countries via the TPP, and India is part of the Asia-wide Regional Comprehensive Economic Partnership negotiations. But India and the United States have no overlap with each other in these efforts. The United States recently expressed support for India's "interest in" APEC membership but stopped short of a declaration of support for India's candidacy and a plan to deliver it. Bilateral investment treaty negotiations are under way but progressing slowly and will not be enough to facilitate faster growth in trade and investment as long as both countries build preferential trade regimes without each other.

On the positive side, science- and technology-based cooperation, though little heralded and underappreciated, has advanced U.S. and Indian shared interests in numerous areas and plays an important role in supporting India's domestic transformation, not least through clean energy, telecommunications leapfrogging, and the rapid growth of the digital economy. More and more, American multinational companies locate research facilities in India, seeing Indian talent as part of their global innovation workforce. The Task Force sees few significant barriers or controversy to continued emphasis on science and technology in bilateral ties, and believes any future government in Washington should encourage strong cooperation in this area.

SHIFT GEARS

Recognizing that India's success is inherently in U.S. interests, the Task Force recommends that Washington and New Delhi transform their economic relationship just as significantly as the civil nuclear agreement transformed their strategic ties in the previous decade. U.S. policymakers should elevate support for India's economic growth and its reform process to the highest bilateral priority, committing to ambitious targets for bilateral economic ties along with clear steps to get there. This will require a shift in U.S. government strategy toward India. Current U.S. economic policy toward India has emphasized the need for India to prove its readiness for high-quality agreements by taking demonstrable steps that signal openness to trade. This approach has not moved the needle in India. Although U.S. officials may see their approach as providing an incentive for India to make changes at home, in practice, the signal has been read in New Delhi as a closed door. Meanwhile, many close U.S. trading partners, such as the European Union, Canada, and Japan, have intensified their trade negotiations with India, even if those discussions will take a long time to conclude.

U.S. policymakers should instead take a strategic approach to economic statecraft with India, providing a high-level commitment to an ambitious trade and economic relationship along with clear steps to get there. The rhetorical U.S. commitment to increase trade flows fivefold, to $500 billion, is helpful in the abstract, but has no specific goalposts for both countries to target. Here, a good precedent can be found in the U.S.-India civil nuclear agreement, which transformed the bilateral relationship, pulled India into the global nonproliferation order, to which it had been an outlier for three decades, and resulted in India harmonizing its domestic laws with global nonproliferation regimes it seeks to enter, such as the Nuclear Suppliers Group and the Missile Technology Control Regime.

After clearly committing to a larger ambition for both countries to work toward, Washington and New Delhi should look for the points of convergence between what Indian officials seek from the United States, what comparative strengths the United States can offer, and what can meet the demands of both countries' political environments. Although India's domestic reforms are in Indian hands, the United States has technical knowledge that can be helpful to India in the process. Looking globally, the United States has an interest in working with New Delhi to ensure that India does not end up an outlier on global trade. And as a tactical matter, a collaborative conversation with a clear and ambitious goal will bring about change more quickly than waiting for India to "prove" itself first.[27]

The United States should commit to ambitious targets for bilateral economic ties along with clear steps to realize them, such as

- leadership of a global diplomatic effort to support India's entry into APEC, and completion of a bilateral investment treaty;
- high-level discussion of bilateral sectoral agreements, such as in services, where India and the United States have more common interests;

- a longer-term pathway to a free-trade agreement or Indian member-ship in an expanded TPP as an equivalent;

- creation of helpful initiatives that respond to Indian interests in domestic reform needs, such as technical advice on market-based approaches to infrastructure financing, or shared work with international financial institutions to reprioritize infrastructure as they once did, as well as continued joint ventures on science and technology, technical cooperation on regulatory reform, bank restructuring, best practices in manufacturing, labor, supply chain, transportation, and vocational skills training, to name a few; and

- continued emphasis on defense trade and technology, a strategic area of cooperation but one that Indian officials largely view in terms of industrial development.

Similarly, the Task Force recommends that the government of India increase the pace and scope of economic liberalization, with the goal of expanding markets, including opening the Indian economy more deeply to trade and foreign investment. The Task Force urges Indian political leaders, in both government and the opposition, to coalesce around a reform agenda, persuade their publics of its urgency, and implement with dispatch. India holds the key to its rise: further unleashing its economy. The Task Force believes strongly that the Indian economy will benefit just as it has over the past fifteen years; as a natural outgrowth, India will be positioned for more substantial ties across the full range of the American economy, not to mention globally. An Indian economy that becomes a significantly larger share of global GDP will make India increasingly indispensable to the rest of the world—a form of power of its own kind. Indian economic leaders have a finely developed understanding of what will propel their economy to the next level and what will make it easier to do business, but they repeatedly find themselves sunk by political problems of execution. Building multiparty constituencies convinced that India's rise depends on further reform now is a choice for Indian leaders to make.

A word about three economic "third rails"—skilled worker visas, a Social Security agreement, and intellectual property rights—also deserves attention. The details of these issues are arcane. On the first two, what India seeks from Washington would require legislation on two of the thorniest domestic policy issues pending before the U.S. Congress and the American public writ large. The stalemate on comprehensive immigration reform in the U.S. Congress severely limits the likelihood of any reform of skilled worker migration policy in the near term. On Social Security, India's system currently does not meet the requirements written into U.S. law for a potential swap (or totalization) agreement. The U.S. Congress is unlikely to write a new law for India, especially when lawmakers have for years refused to approve such an agreement with Mexico, a free-trade partner, which has far more citizens working in the United States, many more U.S. citizens residing in Mexico, and a nearly ten times greater diaspora population in the United States providing a political base for policy support. These twin priorities of the Indian government clash with U.S. law and domestic politics, and are unlikely to be resolved soon. On intellectual property rights, about which many American companies have voiced grievances with India's system, India firmly believes its patent law not only affords access to lifesaving medicines at lower cost but also meets global standards, which a WTO finding recently affirmed. At this point, Indian lawmakers are unlikely to revisit their patent law, especially given the WTO finding. Washington and New Delhi will need to keep open channels of communication on these three issues even while recognizing the political hurdles that prevent easy solutions. These thorny problems should not be allowed to derail progress in other, more productive joint initiatives.

STRATEGIC AND DEFENSE TIES

As noted earlier, U.S.-India defense ties have evolved substantially over the past fifteen years. At one time, U.S. policy toward India focused nearly entirely on nuclear weapons concerns, with Washington and New Delhi on opposite sides of the issue. The civil nuclear agreement changed that. India is now an active strategic partner for the United States in global nonproliferation, and India is now "inside" the global nonproliferation tent. India and the United States have just renewed their framework for defense cooperation and, in a visible step, released the "Joint Strategic Vision for the Asia Pacific and Indian Ocean," formalizing a convergence of views that has now solidified. Indeed, the strategic alignment between India and the United States has become most apparent in the Asia Pacific, where India has become more active, vocally stating its belief in the importance of a rules-based order in the oceans, and strengthening its ties with China, Japan, Korea, Australia, Vietnam, Singapore, and others.

Civilian as well as military consultations now cover the entire globe, although scope exists to routinize these interactions to the level of frequency and informality as exists with the closest U.S. partners. Coordination on humanitarian assistance and disaster relief has expanded, such as with the efforts to assist earthquake victims in Nepal in April 2015. U.S.-India partnership on maritime security has grown significantly, with both sides now discussing collaboration on aircraft carrier technology, to name the most ambitious of an array of new undertakings. Cooperation on high technology coproduction and codevelopment has been progressing, albeit slowly. Finding a better way to calibrate the U.S. bureaucracy for technology licensing alongside the Indian bureaucratic system for equipment procurement will take time, but it will increase the ability of the United States and India to operate together and take on shared missions with greater ease. The linkages among exercises, increased interoperability, and the creation of shared platforms represent tremendous potential for U.S. defense ties with India.

The strategic convergence between Washington and New Delhi on the Asia Pacific should not be construed as an alliance against China. Americans should be careful not to assume that India will play any formal role in hedging China's rise—although India and the United States can help shape the environment in which China makes its choices. Although India has vocally supported Vietnamese and U.S. positions on the South China Sea, the country is too independent, and too proud a power, to be seen as following American strategic plans. In addition, New Delhi has its own particular relations with China, marked by competition and concerns about China's territorial claims to parts of India, but also cooperation, including through shared participation in Asian regional and other organizations such as the BRICS and the Asian Infrastructure Investment Bank, of which the United States is not a member. On the other hand, India's rise—as a model for democracy and pluralism—offers an alternative to the top-down path China has taken and the authoritarianism that appears to be deepening under the current Chinese government. India thus represents an alternative that advances U.S. national interests. A stronger and more powerful India, in and of itself, will offset the emergence of any single dominant power in Asia, an outcome that would be in U.S. interests no matter the nature of New Delhi's ties with Beijing.

Strategically, India also shares Washington's concern about the urgent challenge of Islamic extremism. India has the world's third-largest Muslim population and second-largest Shia population, after Iran. But reports of homegrown terrorism, or Indian Muslims heading off to jihad in the Middle East, remain few and far between. India crafts its Middle East policy with an eye on the home front and is attuned to concerns about domestic blowback, including at the polls. For this reason, in addition to the some seven million Indian-citizen guest workers in the Middle East, India has refrained from joining the international coalition against the Islamic State and has hesitated or urged caution in global security debates about the Arab Spring. Indian officials worry that a more visible counterterrorism posture on groups in the Middle East could bring harm, either in the Middle East itself, where Indian guest workers could be targeted (dozens were kidnapped in the summer of 2014), or at the ballot box in Indian states with large Muslim populations.

In the counterterrorism and law enforcement arena, the United States and India had little cooperation until the Mumbai attacks in 2008, in which Americans were also targeted. A primary plotter of the attack turned out to be a U.S. citizen of Pakistani origin, David Headley, who previously served as a U.S. Drug Enforcement Agency informant. Since then, cooperation has expanded. Still, the **Task Force finds that barriers to a much deeper relationship continue to exist and are tied to U.S. policy toward Pakistan. Indian officials remain skeptical that the United States can ever fully be trusted as a security partner when they see Washington appear to acquiesce to Islamabad's continued inaction on terror groups that have targeted India and the United States. Indian officials also view with skepticism the sale of defense equipment Washington authorizes to Pakistan.** The Lashkar-e-Taiba, responsible for the 2008 Mumbai attacks, operates freely in Pakistan despite the country's declared crackdown on terrorism; its head, an individually designated terrorist under UN sanctions, regularly leads mass public rallies. India sees a seemingly endless stream of U.S. federal dollars supporting defense technology that exceeds what is necessary for counterterror operations and worries that the United States is providing Pakistan with arms it could use against India. If not handled differently, India's suspicion will only become more pronounced with the reduction of U.S. and international troops in Afghanistan in 2017, bringing with it the looming threat of further regional instability.

Pakistan has innumerable problems independent of its issues with India. India is poised for power and prosperity if it can remain focused on its domestic transformation, and the risk of conflict with Pakistan threatens to drag India down. India should not have to, nor should it want to, endure decades further of having its strategic options limited by Pakistan. The United States should encourage India to improve its relationship with Pakistan—as an investment in its own rise—particularly through greater trade connectivity to start, in order to reduce the chances of conflict that could delay or hinder India's global rise. As important, the United States should demand that Pakistan meet its obligations as a state to tackle terrorism emanating from its territory, in both India and Afghanistan. If Pakistan is not willing to rein in terror, Washington should be prepared to end U.S. taxpayer funding for defense equipment sales and coalition support funds reimbursement at minimum.

In addition, the Task Force finds that U.S. policy toward Afghanistan has created particular difficulties in the U.S.-India bilateral relationship due to the increasing threat of greater instability resulting from internal Afghan divisions, the many violent threats to the country's stability, and the drawdown of U.S. and other external forces. New Delhi also fears what it perceives as American eagerness to extricate itself from the region could lead to more influence on the part of China and Pakistan. To New Delhi, that combination appears poised to result in an endgame deal that will seal off Afghanistan from India at the expense of Indian geostrategic equities. Given the increased instability in Afghanistan since the end of the formal international mission there in December 2014, the United States too should worry about Afghanistan returning to a state of chaos, especially in light of developments in Iraq after the departure of U.S. forces—namely, the rise of the self-proclaimed Islamic State. The Task Force recommends that the United States extend its commitment to Afghanistan—even beyond President Obama's decision to slow the withdrawal of U.S. troops from Afghanistan and retain a force of some 5,000 U.S. troops in the country into 2017. The United States should commit to a doctrine stating that future decisions regarding the size, scope, and timeline for deployment of U.S. forces will be determined by on-the-ground realities and not artificially imposed schedules, and without a declared date of departure. Such a move would help assure India and others that U.S. actions will not undermine the goal of long-term regional stability. The United States should also continue to reinforce India's helpful role in development, infrastructure, and diplomacy with Afghanistan, ensuring that India is a standing member of regional consultative mechanisms focused on Afghanistan.

Looking at bilateral strategic ties more generally, **the Task Force finds that defense ties and strategic consultations have progressed well compared with the past but still have much room to grow. Cooperation can develop much further along both the strategic-operational as well as the defense-industrial and technology tracks. Homeland security and technical counterterrorism cooperation has begun but not progressed as deeply as it could.** Initial progress made with the creation of the cabinet-level Homeland Security Dialogue and its working groups has lost momentum and should be reinvigorated. This is among the most promising and vital types of cooperation for both countries, given the challenges of terror in the region and their global reach.

The Task Force recommends that the U.S. government, building on the consultation and increasing levels of interaction of recent years, invest further attention to the security relationship with India across the entire spectrum. Homeland security and counterterrorism cooperation should receive added emphasis. This will mean

- patiently investing in strategic ties with India, deepening consultation frequency and levels of engagement, with an emphasis on the Asia Pacific and the Indian Ocean per the joint strategic vision document;
- facilitating interoperability through exercises, expanding cooperation on maritime domain awareness in the Indian Ocean, and pushing the boundaries of coproduction and codevelopment through the Defense Trade and Technology Initiative;
- **further advancing the prioritization of and attention to homeland security cooperation, which has not met its potential but has never been more urgent,** scaling up the technical-level consultations that bring operational teams—such as experts in megacity policing, port safety and security, countering terrorist financing, countering violent extremism, and supply chain security—together to consult and train;

- deepening consultation with India on **regional nuclear stability**—given concerns about **Pakistan's problems with terrorism, its instability, its nuclear weapons deployment, and its lack of a no-first-use doctrine**—focusing on crisis stability and ensuring that the nuclear taboo remains just that; and

- encouraging a stronger Indian voice and active policy participation on matters of global terrorism and Islamic extremism beyond South Asia while recognizing India's reasons for maintaining a lower public profile.

BILATERAL OPPORTUNITIES ON THE GLOBAL STAGE

The U.S.-India vision statement, crafted at the first Obama-Modi summit in September 2014, asserts a vision for "a partnership in which the United States and India work together, not just for the benefit of both our nations, but for the benefit of the world." The scope of U.S.-India collaboration now cuts across virtually every area, including climate and clean energy, cybersecurity, democracy, development, innovation, health, higher education, science and technology, and women's empowerment. Many of these bilateral collaborations are proceeding rapidly and will likely continue to deliver benefits to the relationship. Some areas, however, despite broad agreement in principle, result in disappointment in Washington due to differences with New Delhi on tactical approaches. The Task Force elected to consider four substantial areas of global cooperation for further discussion: Internet and cybersecurity, global health, clean energy and climate change, and democracy. Two of these, cybersecurity and global health, offer particularly notable potential for U.S.-India joint ventures.

Cyber consultations have expanded in the past half decade despite the Snowden revelations of 2013. India and the United States have increased focus on this critical infrastructure, created a "computer emergency readiness team" agreement with monthly consultation, and share a view of the cyber domain as a commons needing clear rules of the road. But over the past several years, on matters of global Internet governance, Washington has watched with concern as India, where an open Internet has contributed greatly to the flourishing of entrepreneurship and digital economy, appeared to vacillate and even veer toward supporting an intergovernmental governance model. (Indeed, in the words of one Task Force member, India has been seen as the swing state on this global question.) At the Internet Corporation for Assigned Names and Numbers (ICANN) conference in Argentina in June 2015, the Indian government's announcement that it was committed to multistakeholderism provided great relief to many, for India's support will be important to keep the system of Internet governance open in an environment in which countries like Russia and China now push for a stronger governmental role. Still, cyber cooperation with India, like homeland security cooperation, has yet to meet its potential. India possesses one of the world's largest reservoirs of technical capacity in IT, and its clear signal in support of a multistakeholder model opens the door for deepened collaboration on cybersecurity. That includes the matter of Internet governance, where India's commitment to multistakeholderism will have an international effect, as well as more operationally in the law enforcement arena. Cyberattacks, cyberterrorism, strategic threats, and economic cybercrime are all areas of increasing concern to both India and the United States.

Similarly, health has emerged as a quiet but significant area of U.S.-India global cooperation, especially on disease detection and control. The U.S. Centers for Disease Control and Prevention has partnered with the Indian government on a Global Disease Detection Center in India. Governmental, nonprofit, and for-profit efforts cross borders on medical trials, vaccine research and development, and on specific health challenges such as HIV/AIDS, tuberculosis, influenza, and noncommunicable diseases. Given India's large talent pool of medical professionals, including doctors, biologists, nurses, and bioinformatics specialists, much more can be done to advance global health research and response. In addition, India has a growing world-class biotechnology sector and pharmaceutical sector. Indian approaches to innovation are particularly suited to developing world contexts, where fast and effective responses to outbreaks of communicable diseases have never been more important. Indian generic medicines have helped many African countries access lifesaving medicines for patients who otherwise might not be able to afford them.

In cybersecurity and in global health, India has advanced technical capabilities and large, highly capable talent pools with experience working seamlessly with American partners, as has been demonstrated in the private sectors of IT and medical industries.

The Task Force finds that India and the United States have significant common interests—and unique capabilities—in both cyber and health issues, which offer the capacity for potentially transformative bilateral cooperation.

Climate change remains an area in which India and the United States agree in principle on the necessity of action but disagree on the immediacy of next steps. India believes it should be given space to develop its economy before reducing carbon emissions, especially while its per capita emissions remain so much lower than those of developed countries and China. India would like to see developed countries contribute more toward adaptation and mitigation technology. Indian officials are very clear that coal will remain a significant part of their overall energy mix for the future. Those who anticipated that India would follow in China's footsteps by concluding even a modest bilateral agreement on carbon emissions with the United States have been sorely disappointed.

Nevertheless, bilateral cooperation between the United States and India on clean energy has been among the most productive areas in the relationship. India has a rapidly growing renewable energy sector, and the government has more than doubled its targets for solar and wind capacity by 2022. But experts note that improvements in energy efficiency would likely reduce India's emissions even further, and the ramp-up of renewables will not offset India's increasing use of coal in the near term to power its economic growth. In the near term, India's priority on growth will continue to shape political leaders' capacity to slow or limit carbon emissions. Although India's concerns about environmental quality and energy security create an avenue for greater U.S.-India cooperation on emissions reduction, the **Task Force finds little likelihood that India's development pathway and domestic political dynamics would permit the government of India to change its views on a commitment to legally binding emissions frameworks anytime soon.**

Democracy is one of the much-heralded values shared by India and the United States, and one of the reasons Americans find India appealing as a global power and as a partner. Democracy is also under threat in many parts of the world, so there are reasons for hoping to collaborate more intensively with India on democracy worldwide. Yet there are also differences that can surprise. India has been an early and strong supporter of the UN Democracy Fund (UNDEF) and the Community of Democracies. But New Delhi hesitates to criticize lapses in democracy elsewhere. Nor does it proactively promote democracy in the same manner as the United States and European countries, due to India's belief in noninterference. (Although India has, at times, suspended that belief, particularly in issues of urgent regional security in its neighborhood.) India's hesitance to prioritize democracy promotion more actively and human rights concerns as an aspect of democratic health has led to disagreements in critical UN discussions, too. (Of course, Indian observers note American silence on democracy and human rights failings in U.S. allies such as Saudi Arabia and Bahrain.) Finally, India views some of the American focus on democracy promotion as destabilizing, for example in the Middle East. That is one reason why, despite its diplomatic heft and deep stakes in the region, India has said little about the post–Arab Spring crises and has not appeared to endorse any grassroots activism for changes in government in the region.

The Task Force finds that, as the world's two most populous democracies, India and the United States should be obvious partners in work to share lessons from and promote democracy elsewhere in the world. India and the United States should be able to do more together on democracy, but finding the right intersection and comfort level remains a challenge. Technical collaboration may continue to be the most feasible approach given the active Election Commission of India and its capacity to conduct training. Limits will likely remain on India's willingness to comment on uprisings or agitations in other countries, and on actions taken by long-standing strategic partners.

In each of these seemingly discrete areas of global cooperation runs a common thread: India's talent and capacity for technical collaboration. The Task Force has focused its global issues recommendation on leveraging this strength. Collaboration in the cyber arena and global health offer the greatest promise, in the Task Force's view, but climate change and democracy also offer opportunities for technical cooperation that capitalizes on the capacities and talent in both countries. Accordingly, the Task Force recommends the following in these areas:

Cyber domain: **Multilateral Internet governance cooperation has progressed well in 2015 and should continue. On cybersecurity, bilateral collaboration should move beyond consultation to focus on more robust law enforcement cooperation, joint training, warning, and heightened security to continually upgrade protection for this critical infrastructure.**

Health: India is home to low-cost innovation and has been part of the solution in providing access to medicine in the developing world. **As with their collaborations in the clean energy space, India and the United States should create signature joint ventures in global health.** Incentive grants to spur public-private consortia on under-resourced diseases, perhaps for widespread diseases such as malaria or tuberculosis, could be transformational, as could be attention to the growing threat of antibiotic-resistant infections, to name another example where initial work is under way.

Climate change: **Washington should continue to impress on New Delhi the urgency of emissions action, pressing India to commit to improve its energy intensity or declare a per capita income level at which it would be willing to cap emissions if it cannot commit to emissions caps at present. Doing so would signal India's commitment on the world stage. But given India's domestic political constraints, Washington should emphasize collaboration through technical consultation on matters such as grid capacity, energy efficiency, automobile fuel efficiency, and financial tools to mobilize domestic capital for electricity-sector investment. Consultations on civil nuclear energy should continue.** In recognition of the practical reality of India's development pathway, **Washington should revise its policy, which at one time promoted technical assistance for clean coal but no longer does.** These technical efforts will be essentially tweaks at the margins given India's development pathway and its use of coal at scale. India seeks technology to make coal cleaner given that it will be using large aggregate amounts of coal for the foreseeable future. Despite the technical problems involved with clean coal, the United States should be willing to discuss and facilitate technology support to India with the recognition that this is more difficult than it first appears.

Democracy: Respecting their different views on promoting democracy, India and the United States can find ways to work together on the technical building blocks of democracy. Either in bilateral collaboration with India or by supporting India's technical work with democracy-focused institutions such as the International Foundation for Electoral Systems, UNDEF, Community of Democracies, or nongovernmental organizations, **the United States should approach India as a frontline partner on technical training and capacity building for democracy around the world.**

Conclusion

India stands at a moment of potentially significant economic change if it makes the right choices and can forge consensus on its next generation of economic reforms. Although at several points over the past fifteen years India has appeared poised for "takeoff," the prominence of economic growth and job creation on the Modi government's policy agenda departs from previous governments' emphases on welfare programs and offers hope that India's moment may have arrived at last. U.S. policy across four American administrations has supported a more prosperous, more powerful, democratic India as squarely in U.S. national interests for what it would advance economically as well as strategically.

The structural realignment in geopolitics has opened up possibilities for Washington and New Delhi to collaborate more closely. U.S. administrations have worked carefully to craft a new relationship with New Delhi over the past decade, but even after the headlines of bonhomie, sharp difficulties have highlighted the delicacy of the relationship. India has a strong sense of independence and does not seek alliances; working with India hews to no known model of other U.S. partnerships. This Task Force recommends the adoption of a joint-venture framework for conceptualizing how the United States and India should work together, collaborating even more closely on areas of strategic agreement but limiting expectations that India will see eye to eye with Washington on every matter. The joint-venture model accommodates inevitable difficulties by expecting them to exist, making them predictable, and routinizing their management through expanded and more frequent consultation.

Most significantly, the Task Force recommends raising the priority of economic ties with India to the very top of the U.S.-India bilateral agenda, working to develop U.S. support for Indian economic growth, and collaborating actively with India to envision a more ambitious economic goal for Washington and New Delhi with a pathway to get there. An India that can sustain high rates of growth for at least two decades has the ability to transform itself and boost global prosperity, just as China has done. A wealthier India will be a stronger strategic partner, will be able to invest further in its own defense, and will be able to partner more comprehensively across the spectrum of defense and homeland security concerns. India and the United States, although sometimes differing on tactical approaches, have substantial shared interests in global issues, and the Task Force has prioritized pursuit of joint ventures with India in the cyber arena, global health, climate change and clean energy, and democracy.

Given the realignment taking place around the world and India's window for significant change, U.S. interests lie in India realizing that promise for itself and for the benefit of the world, and in ensuring that Washington finds ways to work most productively with this great civilization and rising power.

Additional Views

This report—its findings and recommendations—represents the consensus view of a superb group of Americans with a keen interest in India and our country's relationship with it. Throughout our six months of deliberations, we as a Task Force strived for balance and clear-eyed realism. We looked closely at data, on which we based our findings, and the recommendations flowed from those assessments.

What we did not incorporate, nor comment upon, were less measurable indications of India's trajectory.

My personal view, based on twenty-five years of observation, is unambiguously optimistic about India's future. The India of today would have been completely unimaginable in 1990. A quarter century from now, we will likely say the same. The energy, drive, and most of all ambition that I see and hear from Indian citizens about the kind of country they wish theirs to become—both at home and as a power on the world stage—have already been transformational.

How that change occurs may be slower and with more twists and turns than expected. But I would bet on it.

Alyssa Ayres
joined by Ajay Banga, Marshall M. Bouton, and Sumit Ganguly

While I fully endorse both the overall thrust and the specific recommendations of this excellent report, I believe it is occasionally too restrained in assessing the potential of U.S.-India relations over the long term. The remarkable transformation of the relationship over the last seventeen years and the changed Asian geopolitical situation today, both so well described by the report, call for a more expansive description of future U.S.-India relations than "one of the most substantial opportunities to advance American national interests over the next two decades."

Perhaps this is a purely semantic difference, but I would argue for envisioning, even expecting, that the future will provide one of the two or three greatest opportunities for U.S. foreign policy in that period. The report itself speaks of a process of structural realignment now under way in U.S.-India relations, and there is little to suggest it will not continue, even though the pace and content will be uneven.

Similarly, while I agree with the report's view that the relationship at present is currently best conceived as a set of joint ventures in areas where U.S. and Indian interests align, I would argue that the concept is applied too negatively. Yes, the joint-venture approach will help protect areas of progress from disagreements and disruptions in other areas. But just as companies sometimes begin their cooperation through defined joint ventures and eventually gain the mutual confidence to enter into strategic partnerships, so too is the potential—and perhaps there ought to be the explicit goal—of expanding and building linkages across the joint ventures to the point where that model no longer need apply.

I want to underscore that mine are additional views in line with the report's premises, evidence, and conclusions. I am suggesting merely some greater emphasis on the likely positive long-term trajectory of U.S.-India relations even as I agree that a realistic approach to its current limits is needed.

Marshall M. Bouton
joined by Alyssa Ayres, Ajay Banga, Mary Kissel, and Ashley J. Tellis

I endorse the report with the following comments:

- "Joint venture" should not be seen as a rerun of the relationship between the East India Company and the Mughal Empire; India can certainly protect its own interests in relations with the United States and other major powers. The concept is excellent and has important implications about a limited but expanding partnership.

- In many places, "strategic" should be replaced by "sectoral." The term "strategic relationship" is as fuzzy as "natural ally." Both are examples of diplomatic speak—they conceal more than they reveal and are not useful.

- I disagree with the literal meaning of finding number two: "[N]othing is more important to India's future success—across all facets of national power—than achieving sustained high levels of annual economic growth." India offers the promise of both growth and democracy, and I would not want to see India compromise the latter for the former.

- Finding number eight could be construed as U.S. approval of using any means to end the conflict with Pakistan. It is an invitation to use force, and I do not think this was meant to be the case.

- Finding number nine is overtaken by events—the United States will remain in Afghanistan. I am unaware of any U.S. plan to justify alleged Indian fears of the United States handing off Afghanistan to China and Pakistan. The United States should return to the Bonn process and create a true regional condominium in which India should play a lead role.

- On finding number thirteen, the United States and India should also work with each other to perfect their own democracies, especially in the areas of minority rights, religion and politics, and improving democratic procedures. *Democracy and Diversity: India and the American Experience*, edited by K. Shankar Bajpai, is a model for such discussions; it has important chapters by Indians and Americans.

- Official U.S. policy on Kashmir is now correct and should have been thusly noted, as Kashmir features in every report on India and the region by the Council on Foreign Relations and others. The United States stands ready to help India and Pakistan reach an amicable solution, even an interim one, but only at their joint request.

Stephen P. Cohen

Endnotes

1. United Nations, "The Millennium Development Goals Report 2014," p. 9, http://www. un.org/millenniumgoals/2014%20MDG%20report/MDG%202014%20English%20 web.pdf.

2. See the International Energy Agency, *World Energy Outlook 2014*, http://www. worldenergyoutlook.org.

3. Purchasing power parity, or PPP, compares buying power for a similar basket of goods across vastly different economies. It is not a perfect conversion, and depends on the aggregation of cost data to form usable comparisons. See Angus Deaton and Alan Heston, "Understanding PPPs and PPP-based national accounts," November 2009.

4. For consistency, we use IMF growth rates in this report. India's Central Statistics Office re-based its calculation for India's growth rates in January 2015, resulting in upward revisions for recent years. The bump has raised questions about the data and its interpretation.

5. All GDP data from the World Bank World Development Indicators database, accessed August 18, 2015.

6. See "The 'Bird of Gold': The Rise of India's Consumer Market," McKinsey Global Institute, May 2007; "Special chapter: The Rise of Asia's Middle Class" in *Key Indicators for Asia and the Pacific 2010*, http://www.adb.org/sites/default/files/publication/27726/ ki2010-special-chapter.pdf; Christian Meyer and Nancy Birdsall, "New Estimates of India's Middle Class: Technical Note," Center for Global Development, November 2012, http://www.cgdev.org/doc/2013_MiddleClassIndia_TechnicalNote_CGDNote. pdf; Rakesh Kochhar, "A Global Middle Class Is More Promise Than Reality: From 2001 to 2011, Nearly 700 Million Step Out of Poverty, but Most Only Barely," Pew Research Center, July 2015.

7. U.S. Secretary of Commerce Penny Pritzker, "U.S.-India Commercial and Economic Relationship," address at Carnegie Endowment for International Peace, September 21, 2015, https://www.commerce.gov/news/secretary-speeches/2015/09/ us-secretary-commerce-penny-pritzker-addresses-us-india-commercial.

8. Confederation of Indian Industry and Grant Thornton, "Indian Roots, American Soil: A Survey of Indian Companies' State-by-State Operations in the United States," July 2015, http://online.wsj.com/public/resources/documents/CIIReport.pdf.

9. Government of India, Ministry of Finance, *Economic Survey 2014–15*, vol. II, p.131; "Wasting Time," *Economist*, May 11, 2013, http://www.economist.com/news/ briefing/21577373-india-will-soon-have-fifth-worlds-working-age-population-it-urgently-needs-provide.

10. International Labor Organization, "India: Why Is Women's Labour Force Participation Dropping?" Comment and Analysis, February 13, 2013, http://www.ilo.org/global/ about-the-ilo/newsroom/comment-analysis/WCMS_204762/lang--en/index.htm.

11. "Breaking the Glass Ceiling," *Economist Intelligence Unit*, April 17, 2015, http://country.eiu.com/article.aspx?articleid=123085396.
12. McKinsey Global Institute, "The Power of Parity: How Advancing Women's Equality Can Add \$12 Trillion to Global Growth," September 2015, http://www.mckinsey.com/insights/growth/How_advancing_womens_equality_can_add_12_trillion_to_global_growth. See also the "Third Billion" index from Strategy& (formerly Booz & Company), "Empowering the Third Billion: Women and the World of Work in 2012," http://www.strategyand.pwc.com/media/file/Strategyand_Empowering-the-Third-Billion_Full-Report.pdf.
13. As the study also notes, the estimated costs parallels "what many developing country governments spend on primary education." World Bank, *Voice and Agency: Empowering Women and Girls for Shared Prosperity* (Washington, DC: World Bank Group, 2014), p. 67, http://www.worldbank.org/content/dam/Worldbank/document/Gender/Voice_and_agency_LOWRES.pdf.
14. World Bank, *World DataBank*, Poverty and Equity Database, United States data for 2010, income-based; data for China and India represent 2011 figures and are consumption-based. Separate from the World Bank data, a new study based on Chinese survey data estimates much higher income inequality in China than the consumption-based data suggests—in the range of 53 to 55. See Yu Xie and Xiang Zhou, "Income Inequality in Today's China," *PNAS* vol. 111, no. 19, February 2015, pp. 6928–33, http://www.pnas.org/content/111/19/6928.abstract.
15. On the poverty rate, the *Economic Survey 2014–15* uses statistical data as of the 2011 census.
16. International Monetary Fund, World Economic Outlook database, 2015 data.
17. *Economic Survey 2014–15*, vol. II, p. 6.
18. Ibid., p. 105.
19. C. Fred Bergsten, "India's Rise: A Strategy for Trade-Led Growth," PIIE Briefing no. 15-4, September 2015, http://www.iie.com/publications/briefings/piieb15-4.pdf.
20. For example, the publication in 2012 of *Non-Alignment 2.0*, developed by Indian scholars in dialogue with the then-Indian national security advisor, Shivshankar Menon, and his office, reaffirmed the idea of maximizing India's choices by not tying itself down. See Sunil Khilnani, Rajiv Kumar, Pratap Bhanu Mehta, Prakash Menon, et al., *Non Alignment 2.0, A Foreign and Strategic Policy for India in the Twenty First Century* (New Delhi, Centre for Policy Research, 2012).
21. S. Jaishankar, "Remarks by Foreign Secretary at the Release of Dr. C. Raja Mohan's book, 'Modi's World: Expanding India's Sphere of Influence,'" New Delhi, July 17, 2015, http://mea.gov.in/Speeches-Statements.htm?dtl/25491/Remarks_by_Foreign_Secretary_at_the_release_of_Dr_C_Raja_Mohans_book_Modis_WorldExpanding_Indias_Sphere_of_InfluencequotJuly_17_2015.
22. Dina Smeltz and Ivo Daaldar with Craig Kafura, *Foreign Policy in the Age of Retrenchment: Results of the 2014 Chicago Council Survey of American Public Opinion and U.S. Foreign Policy* (Chicago, Chicago Council on Global Affairs, 2014), p. 35.
23. Dina Smeltz, Ivo Daaldar, Karl Friedhoff, and Craig Kafura, "America Divided: Political Partisanship and U.S. Foreign Policy" (Chicago: Chicago Council on Global Affairs, 2015), pp. 47-48.
24. Bruce Stokes, "The Modi Bounce: Indians Give Their Prime Minister and Economy High Marks, Worry About Crime, Jobs, Prices, Corruption" (Washington, DC, Pew Research Center, September 2015), p. 18.
25. Richard R. Verma, "Recent Developments in the U.S.-India Relations," speech delivered at the Center for Strategic and International Studies, Washington, DC, June 5, 2015.

26. Relevant here is the recommendation of a recent CFR-sponsored Independent Task Force on trade, which noted that the "United States needs a more flexible and varied negotiating strategy that can yield greater market opening in the sectors and countries that promise the largest economic gains." That Task Force urged the United States to "revitalize its trade-negotiating agenda by focusing on the biggest markets and sectors that have the greatest potential for increasing U.S. production of goods and services and for creating additional employment and income in the United States." See Andrew H. Card and Thomas A. Daschle, chairs; Edward Alden and Matthew J. Slaughter, project directors, *U.S. Trade and Investment Policy*, Independent Task Force Report No. 67 (New York: Council on Foreign Relations Press, 2011).

27. This Independent Task Force is not the first to comment upon the limited results of long-standing U.S. trade policy with India. Others have recommended a renewed focus on the bilateral economic relationship as well, including the previously cited C. Fred Bergsten, "India's Rise: A Strategy for Trade-Led Growth," which contains a detailed road map to advance bilateral trade ties. See also Ashley J. Tellis and C. Raja Mohan, "The Strategic Rationale for Deeper U.S.-Indian Economic Ties," Carnegie Endowment for International Peace, 2015. The Asia Society Policy Institute recently launched a multination task force with the express goal of drafting a road map for securing India's membership in APEC.

Task Force Members

Task Force members are asked to join a consensus signifying that they endorse "the general policy thrust and judgments reached by the group, though not necessarily every finding and recommendation." They participate in the Task Force in their individual, not their institutional, capacities.

Alyssa Ayres is senior fellow for India, Pakistan, and South Asia at the Council on Foreign Relations, where she is writing a book about India's rise on the world stage. Ayres served previously as deputy assistant secretary of state for South Asia from 2010 to 2013, covering all issues across a dynamic region of 1.3 billion people (India, Bangladesh, Sri Lanka, Nepal, Maldives, and Bhutan), and providing policy direction for four U.S. embassies and four consulates. Her book on nationalism, culture, and politics in Pakistan, *Speaking Like a State*, was published worldwide by Cambridge University Press in 2009 and received the American Institute of Pakistan Studies Book Prize for 2011–2012. She is also the coeditor of three books on India and Indian foreign policy. At CFR, she focuses on India's role in the world and on the new geopolitics of China, India, and Pakistan. She directs the U.S. Relations with South Asia Roundtable Series and contributes regularly to the *Asia Unbound* blog on CFR.org and to Forbes.com. Ayres has been the recipient of four State Department group or individual Superior Honor Awards. She received an AB magna cum laude from Harvard College, and an MA and PhD from the University of Chicago.

Ajay Banga is president and chief executive officer of MasterCard and a member of its board of directors. Banga is a member of President Barack Obama's Advisory Committee for Trade Policy and Negotiations. He is chairman of the U.S.-India Business Council and a member of the U.S.-India CEO Forum. He is a fellow of the Foreign Policy Association and was awarded the Foreign Policy Association Medal in 2012. Banga serves on the executive committee of the Business Roundtable, and is vice chair of the Financial Services Roundtable as well as the Business Council. He is a member of the International Business Council of the World Economic Forum, CFR, and the Economic Club of New York. Prior to MasterCard, Banga was chief executive officer of Citigroup Asia Pacific. During his career at Citigroup, he held several senior management roles in the United States, Asia Pacific, Europe, Middle East, and Africa. Earlier in his career, Banga worked at Nestlé and PespiCo in India. He is a graduate of Delhi University and the Indian Institute of Management, Ahmedabad.

C. Fred Bergsten is senior fellow and director emeritus at the Peterson Institute for International Economics, having served as the founding director through 2012. He has been the most widely quoted think-tank economist in the world and was called "one of the ten people who can change your life" by *USA Today*. Bergsten was assistant secretary for international affairs at the U.S. Treasury (1977–81), served as undersecretary for monetary affairs (1980–81), and was assistant for international economic affairs to Henry Kissinger at the National Security Council (1969–71). He is a member of President Obama's Advisory Committee for Trade Policy and Negotiations and co-chairman of the Private Sector Advisory Group of the U.S.-India Trade Policy Forum. He is the author, coauthor, or editor of forty-three books on a wide range of international economic issues, including *Bridging the Pacific: Toward Free Trade and Investment Between China and the United States* and *The Long-Term International Economic Position of the United States*. Bergsten has been decorated with the Officer's Cross of the Order of Merit of the Federal Republic of Germany, the Legion of Honor by the government of France, and the Order of the Polar Star by the Government of Sweden. He is an honorary fellow of the Chinese Academy of Social Sciences and was chosen Swedish American of the Year for 2014.

Robert D. Blackwill (member, ex officio) served as dean and faculty member of the Harvard Kennedy School for fourteen years; deputy assistant to the president and deputy national security advisor for strategic planning, presidential envoy to Iraq, and coordinator for U.S. policies regarding Afghanistan and Iran under President George W. Bush; and U.S. ambassador to India from 2001 to 2003. He was special assistant to President George H.W. Bush for European and Soviet affairs, U.S. ambassador to conventional arms negotiations with the Warsaw Pact, director for European affairs at the National Security Council, principal deputy assistant secretary of state for political-military affairs, and principal deputy assistant secretary of state for European affairs. Blackwill is the author of *Revising U.S. Grand Strategy Toward China* and *Lee Kuan Yew: The Grand Master's Insights on China, the United States, and the World* and editor of *Iran: The Nuclear Challenge*. His next book, *War by Other Means: Geoeconomics and Statecraft*, coauthored with Jennifer M. Harris, will be published by Harvard University Press. He is currently the Henry A. Kissinger senior fellow for U.S. foreign policy at CFR.

Marshall M. Bouton is president emeritus of the Chicago Council on Global Affairs, having served as its president from 2001 to 2013. Bouton is currently senior fellow for India with the Asia Society Policy Institute. He also serves as senior fellow at the Center for the Advanced Study of India at the University of Pennsylvania. Bouton speaks and writes frequently on India, Asia, and U.S.-Asia relations. Bouton previously held the position of executive vice president of Asia Society from 1990 to 2001. His earlier positions include director of policy analysis for Near East, Africa, and South Asia at the U.S. Department of Defense, special assistant to the U.S. ambassador to India, and founding U.S. executive secretary of the Indo-U.S. Sub-Commission on Education and Culture. Bouton is coauthor, with Benjamin R. Page, of *The Foreign Policy Disconnect: What Americans Want from Our Leaders but Don't Get*, which was awarded the American Political Science Association's Gladys M. Kammerer Award in 2007. He is the author of *Agrarian Radicalism in South India* and editor/coeditor of several editions of *India Briefing*. He holds an AB cum laude in history from Harvard College, an MA in South Asian studies from the University of Pennsylvania, and a PhD in political science from the University of Chicago.

Nicholas Burns is the Roy and Barbara Goodman family professor of the practice of diplomacy and international relations at the Harvard Kennedy School. He is faculty director of the Future of Diplomacy Project and faculty chair of the programs on the Middle East and South Asia. He is a member of Secretary of State John Kerry's Foreign Affairs Policy Board at the U.S. Department of State, director of the Aspen Strategy Group, and a senior counselor at the Cohen Group. He served in the U.S. Foreign Service for twenty-seven years until his retirement in April 2008. He was undersecretary of state for political affairs from 2005 to 2008. Prior to that, he was ambassador to NATO (2001–2005), ambassador to Greece (1997–2001), and State Department spokesman (1995–97). He worked on the National Security Council staff, where he was senior director for Russia, Ukraine, and Eurasia Affairs and special assistant to President Bill Clinton, and before that, director for Soviet Affairs for President George H.W. Bush. Earlier in his career, he worked at the American Consulate General in Jerusalem and in the American embassies in Egypt and Mauritania. He serves on the board of several corporate and nonprofit organizations.

Stephen P. Cohen is a senior fellow with the India Project in the foreign policy program at the Brookings Institution, following a career as a professor of political science and history at the University of Illinois. In 2004, he was named by the World Affairs Councils of America as one of America's five hundred most influential people in the area of foreign policy. Cohen is the author, coauthor, or editor of more than fourteen books, mostly on South Asian security issues, the most recent being *Shooting for a Century: The India-Pakistan Conundrum* and *The Future of Pakistan*. He has also written books on India, Pakistan, nuclear proliferation, disaster management, and the application of technology to the prevention or amelioration of terrorism. In early 2008, Cohen was a visiting professor at the Lee Kuan Yew School of Public Policy in Singapore, where he taught a course on the politics of manmade and natural disasters. He also taught in Japan at Keio University and in India at Andhra University. He has consulted for numerous foundations and government agencies, and was a member of the policy planning staff at the Department of State from 1985 to 1987. He was a visiting scholar at the Ford Foundation, New Delhi, from 1992 to 1993.

Richard Fontaine is the president of the Center for a New American Security (CNAS). He served as a senior fellow at CNAS from 2009 to 2012 and previously as foreign policy advisor to Senator John McCain. He has also worked at the State Department and the National Security Council (NSC) and on the staff of the Senate Foreign Relations Committee. Fontaine served as foreign policy advisor to the McCain 2008 presidential campaign and, following the election, as the minority deputy staff director on the Senate Armed Services Committee. Prior to this, he served as associate director for Near Eastern affairs at the NSC from 2003 to 2004 and also worked in the NSC's Asian Affairs directorate. During his time at the State Department, Fontaine worked in the office of the deputy secretary of state and in the department's South Asia bureau, working on issues related to India, Nepal, and Sri Lanka. Fontaine began his foreign policy career as a staff member of the Senate Foreign Relations Committee, focusing on the Middle East and South Asia. Fontaine graduated summa cum laude with a BA in international relations from Tulane University and holds an MA in international affairs from Johns Hopkins University's School of Advanced International Studies. He is a member of the Council on Foreign Relations and has been an adjunct professor at Georgetown University.

Sumit Ganguly is a professor of political science and the director of the Center on American and Global Security, and holds the Rabindranath Tagore chair in Indian cultures and civilizations at Indiana University, Bloomington. Ganguly is the founding editor of the *India Review*, the only refereed journal in North America devoted to the study of contemporary Indian politics, economics, and society. He serves on the editorial boards of multiple professional journals, including the *American Political Science Review*, *Current History*, *International Security*, *Journal of Democracy*, and *Pacific Affairs*. He is also the coeditor, with Srinath Sreenivasan, of the Oxford International Relations of South Asia book series through Oxford University Press/New Delhi. His most recent book is the *Oxford Short Introduction to Indian Foreign Policy*. In 2016, Yale University Press will publish his coauthored book with William R. Thompson, *Ascending India and Its State Capacity*. Additionally, next spring Cambridge University Press will publish his book *Deadly Impasse: India and Pakistan at the Dawn of New Century*. He is also the recipient of the triannual J. David Singer Award from the Midwest Section of the International Studies Association for his book with Karen Rasler and William R. Thompson, *How Rivalries End*.

Helene D. Gayle is chief executive officer of McKinsey Social Initiative, a nonprofit organization that implements programs that bring together varied stakeholders to address complex global social challenges. Previously, she was president and chief executive officer of CARE USA, a leading international humanitarian organization. An expert on global development, humanitarian, and health issues, she spent twenty years

with the Centers for Disease Control and Prevention, working primar-
ily on HIV/AIDS. Gayle then worked at the Bill and Melinda Gates
Foundation, directing programs on HIV/AIDS and other global health
issues. She serves on the boards of the Coca-Cola Company, Colgate-
Palmolive Company, Rockefeller Foundation, Center for Strategic and
International Studies, New America Foundation, ONE Campaign, and
the Atlanta Metro Chamber of Commerce, and also serves on the President's Commission on White House Fellowships. She is a member of
the Council on Foreign Relations, American Public Health Association,
Institute of Medicine, and American Academy of Pediatrics. Named
one of *Forbes*' 100 Most Powerful Women, she has authored numerous articles on global and domestic public health issues, poverty alle-
viation, gender equality, and social justice. Gayle was born and raised
in Buffalo, New York. She earned a BA in psychology at Barnard College, an MD from the University of Pennsylvania, and an MPH from
Johns Hopkins University. She has received thirteen honorary degrees
and holds faculty appointments at the University of Washington and
Emory University.

Charles R. Kaye, co-chief executive officer of Warburg Pincus, has
been with the company since 1986 and has been jointly responsible
for the management of the firm since 2000. Kaye lived in Hong Kong
from 1994 to 1999, where he was instrumental in the launch and development of Warburg Pincus' Asia operations. Kaye is a graduate of the
University of Texas, a member of the Council on Foreign Relations, and
co-chairman of the Partnership Fund for New York City and the international advisory board of the Center for the Advanced Study of India.
He is the former chairman of the U.S.-India Business Council and the
Asia Society. Kaye is also an investment committee member of Sheri-
dan Production Partners.

Mary Kissel is a *Wall Street Journal* editorial board member, where she
comments on politics and policy in the unsigned Review & Outlook
column, and the host of Opinion Journal on WSJ Video. She is also a
weekly cohost of the nationally syndicated *John Batchelor Show*, a conservative radio news magazine. Kissel joined the *Wall Street Journal* in
Hong Kong in 2004 as a financial columnist and served as Asia opinion
editor from 2005 to 2010, directing the newspaper's commentary on
more than twenty countries. Previously, she worked at Goldman Sachs

in New York and London. Kissel's work has appeared in the *Far Eastern Economic Review*, *World Affairs*, and *Spectator Australia*, among other publications. Her radio and television credentials include Australian Broadcasting, BBC, CNN, Fox Business, and Fox News. Kissel holds a a bachelor's degree in government from Harvard College and master's degree in international affairs from Johns Hopkins University's School of Advanced International Studies.

Joseph S. Nye Jr. is university distinguished service professor and former dean of the Harvard Kennedy School. He received his bachelor's degree summa cum laude from Princeton University, studied at Oxford University on a Rhodes scholarship, and earned a doctorate in political science from Harvard, where he joined the faculty in 1964. In 2008, a poll of 2,700 international relations scholars listed him as the most influential scholar on American foreign policy, and in 2011 *Foreign Policy* listed him among the "100 leading global thinkers." From 1977 to 1979, Nye was a deputy undersecretary of state and chaired the National Security Council group on nonproliferation of nuclear weapons. He chaired the National Intelligence Council from 1993 to 1994, and served as assistant secretary of defense for international security affairs from 1994 to 1995. He won distinguished service medals from all three agencies. Nye has published fourteen academic books, a novel, and more than 150 articles in professional and policy journals. Recent books include *Soft Power*, *The Powers to Lead*, *The Future of Power*, and *Is the American Century Over?* He is a fellow of the American Academy of Arts and Sciences, British Academy, and American Academy of Diplomacy, and an honorary fellow of Exeter College, Oxford. He is the recipient of Princeton University's Woodrow Wilson Award, the Charles Merriam Award from the American Political Science Association, France's Palmes Academiques, and various honorary degrees.

Gary Roughead (U.S. Navy, retired) served as the U.S. Navy's twenty-ninth chief of naval operations after holding six operational commands, and is one of only two officers in the history of the navy to have commanded both the U.S. Atlantic and Pacific Fleets. As the chief of naval operations, Roughead led the navy through a challenging period of transition in fiscal, security, and personnel matters. He accelerated the navy's capability and capacity in ballistic missile defense and unmanned air and underwater systems. He reestablished the Fourth and Tenth Fleets to better focus on the Western Hemisphere and cyber operations, respectively, and introduced programs to prepare for the primacy of information in warfare. In retirement, Roughead is an Annenberg distinguished fellow at the Hoover Institution at Stanford University and serves on the boards of directors of the Northrop Grumman Corporation, Theranos, Inc., and the Center for a New American Security. He is a trustee of Dodge and Cox Funds and serves on the board of managers of the Johns Hopkins University Applied Physics Laboratory. He advises companies in the national security and medical sectors.

Mariko Silver is the tenth president of Bennington College, a liberal arts college distinguished for its pioneering initiatives in higher education. Silver was acting assistant secretary for international affairs and deputy assistant secretary for international policy in the Department of Homeland Security under President Barack Obama, where she helped spearhead the creation of the first U.S.-India Homeland Security Dialogue. She served as policy advisor for innovation, higher education, and economic development in the administration of former Arizona Governor Janet Napolitano. She has also held positions at Arizona State University and Columbia University, where she advanced a range of initiatives in international education cooperation and science and technology-driven economic development. Silver holds a BA in history from Yale University, an MSc in Science and Technology Policy from the University of Sussex in the United Kingdom, and a PhD in economic geography from the University of California, Los Angeles.

Ashley J. Tellis is a senior associate at the Carnegie Endowment for International Peace specializing in international security, defense, and Asian strategic issues. While on assignment to the U.S. Department of State as senior advisor to the undersecretary of state for political affairs, he was intimately involved in negotiating the civil nuclear agreement with India. Previously, he was commissioned into the U.S. Foreign Service and served as senior advisor to the ambassador at the U.S. embassy in New Delhi. He also served on the National Security Council staff as special assistant to the president and senior director for strategic planning and Southwest Asia. Prior to his government service, Tellis was senior policy analyst at the RAND Corporation and professor of policy analysis at the RAND Graduate School. He is the author of *India's*

Emerging Nuclear Posture: Between Recessed Deterrent and Ready Arsenal and coauthor of *Interpreting China's Grand Strategy: Past, Present, and Future.* He is the research director of the Strategic Asia Program at the National Bureau of Asian Research and coeditor of the program's eleven most recent annual volumes, including this year's *Strategic Asia 2014–15: U.S. Alliances and Partnerships at the Center of Global Power.*

Task Force Observers

Observers participate in Task Force discussions, but are not asked to join the consensus. They participate in their individual, not institutional, capacities.

Thomas J. Bollyky is the senior fellow for global health, economics, and development at the Council on Foreign Relations. He is also an adjunct professor of law at Georgetown University. Prior to coming to CFR, Bollyky was a fellow at the Center for Global Development and director of intellectual property and innovation at the Office of the U.S. Trade Representative (USTR), where he led the negotiations for medical technologies in the U.S.-Republic of Korea Free Trade Agreement and represented USTR in the negotiations with China on the safety of food and drug imports. He was a Fulbright scholar to South Africa, where he worked as a staff attorney at the AIDS Law Project on treatment access issues related to HIV/AIDS, and an attorney at Debevoise & Plimpton LLP. Bollyky has testified multiple times before the U.S. Senate, and his work has appeared in the *New York Times*, *Science*, *Foreign Affairs*, the *Journal of the American Medical Association*, the *Atlantic*, and the *Lancet*. He is a member of the advisory committee for the Clinton Global Initiative and has served as a consultant to the Bill and Melinda Gates Foundation. Bollyky received his BA in biology and history from Columbia University and his JD from Stanford Law School. In 2013, the World Economic Forum named Bollyky as one of its global leaders under forty.

Michael A. Levi is the David M. Rubenstein senior fellow for energy and the environment at the Council on Foreign Relations and director of CFR's Maurice R. Greenberg Center for Geoeconomic Studies. He is an expert on domestic and international energy markets and policy, climate change, and nuclear security. Levi is author of four books, most recently *The Power Surge: Energy, Opportunity, and the Battle for America's Future*, which explored the drivers and consequences of two emerging revolutions in American energy, and *By All Means Necessary: How China's Resource Quest Is Changing the World* (with Elizabeth C. Economy), which investigated Chinese efforts to secure natural resources, including in North America. He is a member of the advisory board to Princeton University's Carbon Mitigation Initiative and a member of the strategic advisory board for NewWorld Capital LLC. Before joining CFR, Levi was a science fellow in foreign policy studies at the Brookings Institution. Levi holds an MA in physics from Princeton University and a PhD in war studies from the University of London (King's College).

Daniel S. Markey is senior research professor at Johns Hopkins University's School of Advanced International Studies (SAIS). He is also the academic director for the SAIS Global Policy Program and an adjunct senior fellow for India, Pakistan, and South Asia at the Council on Foreign Relations. From 2007 to 2015, Markey was senior fellow for India, Pakistan, and South Asia at CFR. While there, he wrote a book on the future of the U.S.-Pakistan relationship, *No Exit from Pakistan: America's Tortured Relationship with Islamabad*. From 2003 to 2007, Markey held the South Asia portfolio on the secretary's policy planning staff at the U.S. Department of State. Prior to government service, he taught in the department of politics at Princeton University, and served as executive director of Princeton's research program in international security. Earlier, he was a postdoctoral fellow at Harvard's Olin Institute for Strategic Studies. Markey is the author of numerous reports, articles, book chapters, and opinion pieces. In 2010, he served as project director of the CFR-sponsored Independent Task Force on U.S. strategy in Pakistan and Afghanistan. Markey earned a bachelor's degree from Johns Hopkins University and a doctorate in politics from Princeton University.

Damian Murphy is a senior professional staff member on the Senate Foreign Relations Committee minority side, focused on Europe and South and Central Asia. For four years, he was the senior policy advisor for foreign policy, national security, and homeland security for Senator Bob Casey (D-PA), former chairman of the subcommittee on Near Eastern and South and Central Asian affairs. Previously, Murphy managed Freedom House programs in Central and Eastern Europe and conducted its congressional outreach. Prior to that, he was the national field director for the U.S. Global Leadership Campaign, a coalition of businesses and NGOs that advocate for funding for international affairs. He worked at the National Democratic Institute for International Affairs for five years on democratic development projects in the Balkans, East Africa, Middle East, and East Asia. Murphy has a degree in world politics from the Catholic University of America and a master's degree in international security studies from Georgetown University. Murphy is a Truman National Security fellow.

Neena Shenai is principal global trade counsel for Medtronic. She formerly served as trade counsel for the Committee on Ways and Means in the U.S. House of Representatives with Chairmen Paul Ryan and Dave Camp. Previously, Shenai served as banking, commerce, transportation, and trade counsel for the Senate Republican Policy Committee; research fellow at the American Enterprise Institute; senior advisor for the Bureau of Industry and Security of the U.S. Department of Commerce; an attorney in the international trade group of Skadden, Arps, Slate, Meagher & Flom; a professional trainee in the rules division of the World Trade Organization; and a judicial law clerk for the Honorable Evan J. Wallach, U.S. Court of International Trade. Shenai has a BA with high honors from Swarthmore College, an MPhil in international relations from St. Antony's College, Oxford University, and a JD from Vanderbilt University.

Varun Sivaram is the Douglas Dillon fellow at the Council on Foreign Relations. He is also a strategic advisor to the office of New York Governor Andrew Cuomo on Reforming the Energy Vision. Before joining CFR, he was a consultant at McKinsey and Company, where he counseled Fortune 500 companies on adapting to the modern competitive landscape in energy. Prior to this role, he served as a senior advisor for energy and water policy to the mayor of Los Angeles, Antonio Villaraigosa, and oversaw the city's department of water and power. His work has appeared in the *Journal of Applied Physics*, *Journal of Physical Chemistry*, *Nature*, *Nature Climate Change*, *Scientific American*, and the World Economic Forum. A Truman and a Rhodes scholar, Sivaram holds degrees from Stanford University in engineering physics and international relations, with honors in international security. He holds a PhD in condensed matter physics from St. John's College, Oxford University, where he developed third-generation solar photovoltaic coatings for building-integrated applications. He lives in Washington, DC.

Rachel B. Vogelstein is a senior fellow and director of the Women and Foreign Policy Program at the Council on Foreign Relations in Washington, DC. She is also a professor of gender and U.S. foreign policy at Georgetown Law School. From 2009 to 2012, Vogelstein was director of policy and senior advisor in the Office of Global Women's Issues under Secretary of State Hillary Rodham Clinton at the U.S. Department of State. She also represented the State Department as a member of the White House Council on Women and Girls. Following her tenure at the State Department, she served as the director of women's and girls' programs in the Office of Hillary Rodham Clinton at the Clinton Foundation, where she oversaw the development of the No Ceilings initiative and provided guidance on domestic and global women's issues. Vogelstein is an attorney by training, with expertise on gender equality. She has lectured widely on the rights of women and girls, including at the U.S. Congressional Women's Caucus, U.S. Department of State, U.S. Foreign Service Institute, the World Bank, and Harvard Law School. She holds a BA from Barnard College, Columbia University, and a JD from Georgetown Law School.

Independent Task Force Reports

Published by the Council on Foreign Relations

The Emerging Global Health Crisis: Noncommunicable Diseases in Low- and Middle-Income Countries
Mitchell E. Daniels Jr. and Thomas E. Donilon, Chairs; Thomas J. Bollyky, Project Director
Independent Task Force Report No. 72 (2014)

North America: Time for a New Focus
David H. Petraeus and Robert B. Zoellick, Chairs; Shannon K. O'Neil, Project Director
Independent Task Force No. 71 (2014)

Defending an Open, Global, Secure, and Resilient Internet
John D. Negroponte and Samuel J. Palmisano, Chairs; Adam Segal, Project Director
Independent Task Force Report No. 70 (2013)

U.S.-Turkey Relations: A New Partnership
Madeleine K. Albright and Stephen J. Hadley, Chairs; Steven A. Cook, Project Director
Independent Task Force Report No. 69 (2012)

U.S. Education Reform and National Security
Joel I. Klein and Condoleezza Rice, Chairs; Julia Levy, Project Director
Independent Task Force Report No. 68 (2012)

U.S. Trade and Investment Policy
Andrew H. Card and Thomas A. Daschle, Chairs; Edward Alden and Matthew J. Slaughter, Project Directors
Independent Task Force Report No. 67 (2011)

Global Brazil and U.S.-Brazil Relations
Samuel W. Bodman and James D. Wolfensohn, Chairs; Julia E. Sweig, Project Director
Independent Task Force Report No. 66 (2011)

U.S. Strategy for Pakistan and Afghanistan
Richard L. Armitage and Samuel R. Berger, Chairs; Daniel S. Markey, Project Director
Independent Task Force Report No. 65 (2010)

U.S. Policy Toward the Korean Peninsula
Charles L. Pritchard and John H. Tilelli Jr., Chairs; Scott A. Snyder, Project Director
Independent Task Force Report No. 64 (2010)

U.S. Immigration Policy
Jeb Bush and Thomas F. McLarty III, Chairs; Edward Alden, Project Director
Independent Task Force Report No. 63 (2009)

U.S. Nuclear Weapons Policy
William J. Perry and Brent Scowcroft, Chairs; Charles D. Ferguson, Project Director
Independent Task Force Report No. 62 (2009)

Confronting Climate Change: A Strategy for U.S. Foreign Policy
George E. Pataki and Thomas J. Vilsack, Chairs; Michael A. Levi, Project Director
Independent Task Force Report No. 61 (2008)

U.S.-Latin America Relations: A New Direction for a New Reality
Charlene Barshefsky and James T. Hill, Chairs; Shannon O'Neil, Project Director
Independent Task Force Report No. 60 (2008)

U.S.-China Relations: An Affirmative Agenda, A Responsible Course
Carla A. Hills and Dennis C. Blair, Chairs; Frank Sampson Jannuzi, Project Director
Independent Task Force Report No. 59 (2007)

National Security Consequences of U.S. Oil Dependency
John Deutch and James R. Schlesinger, Chairs; David G. Victor, Project Director
Independent Task Force Report No. 58 (2006)

Russia's Wrong Direction: What the United States Can and Should Do
John Edwards and Jack Kemp, Chairs; Stephen Sestanovich, Project Director
Independent Task Force Report No. 57 (2006)

More than Humanitarianism: A Strategic U.S. Approach Toward Africa
Anthony Lake and Christine Todd Whitman, Chairs; Princeton N. Lyman and J. Stephen
Morrison, Project Directors
Independent Task Force Report No. 56 (2006)

In the Wake of War: Improving Post-Conflict Capabilities
Samuel R. Berger and Brent Scowcroft, Chairs; William L. Nash, Project Director; Mona K.
Sutphen, Deputy Director
Independent Task Force Report No. 55 (2005)

In Support of Arab Democracy: Why and How
Madeleine K. Albright and Vin Weber, Chairs; Steven A. Cook, Project Director
Independent Task Force Report No. 54 (2005)

Building a North American Community
John P. Manley, Pedro Aspe, and William F. Weld, Chairs; Thomas d'Aquino, Andrés
Rozental, and Robert Pastor, Vice Chairs; Chappell H. Lawson, Project Director
Independent Task Force Report No. 53 (2005)

Iran: Time for a New Approach
Zbigniew Brzezinski and Robert M. Gates, Chairs; Suzanne Maloney, Project Director
Independent Task Force Report No. 52 (2004)

An Update on the Global Campaign Against Terrorist Financing
Maurice R. Greenberg, Chair; William F. Wechsler and Lee S. Wolosky, Project Directors
Independent Task Force Report No. 40B (Web-only release, 2004)

Renewing the Atlantic Partnership
Henry A. Kissinger and Lawrence H. Summers, Chairs; Charles A. Kupchan, Project Director
Independent Task Force Report No. 51 (2004)

Iraq: One Year After
Thomas R. Pickering and James R. Schlesinger, Chairs; Eric P. Schwartz, Project Consultant
Independent Task Force Report No. 43C (Web-only release, 2004)

Nonlethal Weapons and Capabilities
Paul X. Kelley and Graham Allison, Chairs; Richard L. Garwin, Project Director
Independent Task Force Report No. 50 (2004)

New Priorities in South Asia: U.S. Policy Toward India, Pakistan, and Afghanistan (Chairmen's Report)
Marshall Bouton, Nicholas Platt, and Frank G. Wisner, Chairs; Dennis Kux and Mahnaz Ispahani, Project Directors
Independent Task Force Report No. 49 (2003)
Cosponsored with the Asia Society

Finding America's Voice: A Strategy for Reinvigorating U.S. Public Diplomacy
Peter G. Peterson, Chair; Kathy Bloomgarden, Henry Grunwald, David E. Morey, and Shibley Telhami, Working Committee Chairs; Jennifer Sieg, Project Director; Sharon Herbstman, Project Coordinator
Independent Task Force Report No. 48 (2003)

Emergency Responders: Drastically Underfunded, Dangerously Unprepared
Warren B. Rudman, Chair; Richard A. Clarke, Senior Adviser; Jamie F. Metzl, Project Director
Independent Task Force Report No. 47 (2003)

Iraq: The Day After (Chairs' Update)
Thomas R. Pickering and James R. Schlesinger, Chairs; Eric P. Schwartz, Project Director
Independent Task Force Report No. 43B (Web-only release, 2003)

Burma: Time for Change
Mathea Falco, Chair
Independent Task Force Report No. 46 (2003)

Afghanistan: Are We Losing the Peace?
Marshall Bouton, Nicholas Platt, and Frank G. Wisner, Chairs; Dennis Kux and Mahnaz Ispahani, Project Directors
Chairman's Report of an Independent Task Force (2003)
Cosponsored with the Asia Society

Meeting the North Korean Nuclear Challenge
Morton I. Abramowitz and James T. Laney, Chairs; Eric Heginbotham, Project Director
Independent Task Force Report No. 45 (2003)

Chinese Military Power
Harold Brown, Chair; Joseph W. Prueher, Vice Chair; Adam Segal, Project Director
Independent Task Force Report No. 44 (2003)

Iraq: The Day After
Thomas R. Pickering and James R. Schlesinger, Chairs; Eric P. Schwartz, Project Director
Independent Task Force Report No. 43 (2003)

Threats to Democracy: Prevention and Response
Madeleine K. Albright and Bronislaw Geremek, Chairs; Morton H. Halperin, Director;
Elizabeth Frawley Bagley, Associate Director
Independent Task Force Report No. 42 (2002)

America—Still Unprepared, Still in Danger
Gary Hart and Warren B. Rudman, Chairs; Stephen E. Flynn, Project Director
Independent Task Force Report No. 41 (2002)

Terrorist Financing
Maurice R. Greenberg, Chair; William F. Wechsler and Lee S. Wolosky, Project Directors
Independent Task Force Report No. 40 (2002)

Enhancing U.S. Leadership at the United Nations
David Dreier and Lee H. Hamilton, Chairs; Lee Feinstein and Adrian Karatnycky, Project
Directors
Independent Task Force Report No. 39 (2002)
Cosponsored with Freedom House

Improving the U.S. Public Diplomacy Campaign in the War Against Terrorism
Carla A. Hills and Richard C. Holbrooke, Chairs; Charles G. Boyd, Project Director
Independent Task Force Report No. 38 (Web-only release, 2001)

Building Support for More Open Trade
Kenneth M. Duberstein and Robert E. Rubin, Chairs; Timothy F. Geithner, Project Director;
Daniel R. Lucich, Deputy Project Director
Independent Task Force Report No. 37 (2001)

Beginning the Journey: China, the United States, and the WTO
Robert D. Hormats, Chair; Elizabeth Economy and Kevin Nealer, Project Directors
Independent Task Force Report No. 36 (2001)

Strategic Energy Policy Update
Edward L. Morse, Chair; Amy Myers Jaffe, Project Director
Independent Task Force Report No. 33B (2001)
Cosponsored with the James A. Baker III Institute for Public Policy of Rice University

Testing North Korea: The Next Stage in U.S. and ROK Policy
Morton I. Abramowitz and James T. Laney, Chairs; Robert A. Manning, Project Director
Independent Task Force Report No. 35 (2001)

The United States and Southeast Asia: A Policy Agenda for the New Administration
J. Robert Kerrey, Chair; Robert A. Manning, Project Director
Independent Task Force Report No. 34 (2001)

Strategic Energy Policy: Challenges for the 21st Century
Edward L. Morse, Chair; Amy Myers Jaffe, Project Director
Independent Task Force Report No. 33 (2001)
Cosponsored with the James A. Baker III Institute for Public Policy of Rice University

A Letter to the President and a Memorandum on U.S. Policy Toward Brazil
Stephen Robert, Chair; Kenneth Maxwell, Project Director
Independent Task Force Report No. 32 (2001)

State Department Reform
Frank C. Carlucci, Chair; Ian J. Brzezinski, Project Coordinator
Independent Task Force Report No. 31 (2001)
Cosponsored with the Center for Strategic and International Studies

U.S.-Cuban Relations in the 21st Century: A Follow-on Report
Bernard W. Aronson and William D. Rogers, Chairs; Julia Sweig and Walter Mead, Project Directors
Independent Task Force Report No. 30 (2000)

Toward Greater Peace and Security in Colombia: Forging a Constructive U.S. Policy
Bob Graham and Brent Scowcroft, Chairs; Michael Shifter, Project Director
Independent Task Force Report No. 29 (2000)
Cosponsored with the Inter-American Dialogue

Future Directions for U.S. Economic Policy Toward Japan
Laura D'Andrea Tyson, Chair; M. Diana Helweg Newton, Project Director
Independent Task Force Report No. 28 (2000)

First Steps Toward a Constructive U.S. Policy in Colombia
Bob Graham and Brent Scowcroft, Chairs; Michael Shifter, Project Director
Interim Report (2000)
Cosponsored with the Inter-American Dialogue

Promoting Sustainable Economies in the Balkans
Steven Rattner, Chair; Michael B.G. Froman, Project Director
Independent Task Force Report No. 27 (2000)

Non-Lethal Technologies: Progress and Prospects
Richard L. Garwin, Chair; W. Montague Winfield, Project Director
Independent Task Force Report No. 26 (1999)

Safeguarding Prosperity in a Global Financial System:
The Future International Financial Architecture
Carla A. Hills and Peter G. Peterson, Chairs; Morris Goldstein, Project Director
Independent Task Force Report No. 25 (1999)
Cosponsored with the International Institute for Economics

U.S. Policy Toward North Korea: Next Steps
Morton I. Abramowitz and James T. Laney, Chairs; Michael J. Green, Project Director
Independent Task Force Report No. 24 (1999)

Reconstructing the Balkans
Morton I. Abramowitz and Albert Fishlow, Chairs; Charles A. Kupchan, Project Director
Independent Task Force Report No. 23 (Web-only release, 1999)

Strengthening Palestinian Public Institutions
Michel Rocard, Chair; Henry Siegman, Project Director; Yezid Sayigh and Khalil Shikaki,
Principal Authors
Independent Task Force Report No. 22 (1999)

U.S. Policy Toward Northeastern Europe
Zbigniew Brzezinski, Chair; F. Stephen Larrabee, Project Director
Independent Task Force Report No. 21 (1999)

The Future of Transatlantic Relations
Robert D. Blackwill, Chair and Project Director
Independent Task Force Report No. 20 (1999)

U.S.-Cuban Relations in the 21st Century
Bernard W. Aronson and William D. Rogers, Chairs; Walter Russell Mead, Project Director
Independent Task Force Report No. 19 (1999)

After the Tests: U.S. Policy Toward India and Pakistan
Richard N. Haass and Morton H. Halperin, Chairs
Independent Task Force Report No. 18 (1998)
Cosponsored with the Brookings Institution

Managing Change on the Korean Peninsula
Morton I. Abramowitz and James T. Laney, Chairs; Michael J. Green, Project Director
Independent Task Force Report No. 17 (1998)

Promoting U.S. Economic Relations with Africa
Peggy Dulany and Frank Savage, Chairs; Salih Booker, Project Director
Independent Task Force Report No. 16 (1998)

U.S. Middle East Policy and the Peace Process
Henry Siegman, Project Coordinator
Independent Task Force Report No. 15 (1997)

Differentiated Containment: U.S. Policy Toward Iran and Iraq
Zbigniew Brzezinski and Brent Scowcroft, Chairs; Richard W. Murphy, Project Director
Independent Task Force Report No. 14 (1997)

Russia, Its Neighbors, and an Enlarging NATO
Richard G. Lugar, Chair; Victoria Nuland, Project Director
Independent Task Force Report No. 13 (1997)

Rethinking International Drug Control: New Directions for U.S. Policy
Mathea Falco, Chair
Independent Task Force Report No. 12 (1997)

Financing America's Leadership: Protecting American Interests and Promoting American Values
Mickey Edwards and Stephen J. Solarz, Chairs; Morton H. Halperin, Lawrence J. Korb,
and Richard M. Moose, Project Directors
Independent Task Force Report No. 11 (1997)
Cosponsored with the Brookings Institution

A New U.S. Policy Toward India and Pakistan
Richard N. Haass, Chair; Gideon Rose, Project Director
Independent Task Force Report No. 10 (1997)

Arms Control and the U.S.-Russian Relationship
Robert D. Blackwill, Chair and Author; Keith W. Dayton, Project Director
Independent Task Force Report No. 9 (1996)
Cosponsored with the Nixon Center for Peace and Freedom

American National Interest and the United Nations
George Soros, Chair
Independent Task Force Report No. 8 (1996)

Making Intelligence Smarter: The Future of U.S. Intelligence
Maurice R. Greenberg, Chair; Richard N. Haass, Project Director
Independent Task Force Report No. 7 (1996)

Lessons of the Mexican Peso Crisis
John C. Whitehead, Chair; Marie-Josée Kravis, Project Director
Independent Task Force Report No. 6 (1996)

Managing the Taiwan Issue: Key Is Better U.S. Relations with China
Stephen Friedman, Chair; Elizabeth Economy, Project Director
Independent Task Force Report No. 5 (1995)

Non-Lethal Technologies: Military Options and Implications
Malcolm H. Wiener, Chair
Independent Task Force Report No. 4 (1995)

Should NATO Expand?
Harold Brown, Chair; Charles A. Kupchan, Project Director
Independent Task Force Report No. 3 (1995)

Success or Sellout? The U.S.-North Korean Nuclear Accord
Kyung Won Kim and Nicholas Platt, Chairs; Richard N. Haass, Project Director
Independent Task Force Report No. 2 (1995)
Cosponsored with the Seoul Forum for International Affairs

Nuclear Proliferation: Confronting the New Challenges
Stephen J. Hadley, Chair; Mitchell B. Reiss, Project Director
Independent Task Force Report No. 1 (1995)

Note: Task Force reports are available for download from CFR's website, www.cfr.org.
For more information, email publications@cfr.org.